MAD LIBS®

MAD LIBS MANIA

MAD LIBS®

MAD LIBS MANIA

MAD LIBS
An Imprint of Penguin Random House LLC

Concept created by Roger Price & Leonard Stern

Mad Libs Mania published in 2015 by Mad Libs,
an imprint of Penguin Random House LLC, New York.
Printed in the USA.

Visit us online at penguinrandomhouse.com

Mad Libs Mania ISBN 9780843182897
25 27 29 31 33 34 32 30 28 26 24

MAD LIBS®

GRAB BAG
MAD LIBS

by Roger Price and Leonard Stern

MAD LIBS

INSTRUCTIONS

MAD LIBS® is a game for people who don't like games!
It can be played by one, two, three, four, or forty.

● RIDICULOUSLY SIMPLE DIRECTIONS

In this tablet you will find stories containing blank spaces where words are left out. One player, the READER, selects one of these stories. The READER does not tell anyone what the story is about. Instead, he/she asks the other players, the WRITERS, to give him/her words. These words are used to fill in the blank spaces in the story.

● TO PLAY

The READER asks each WRITER in turn to call out a word—an adjective or a noun or whatever the space calls for—and uses them to fill in the blank spaces in the story. The result is a MAD LIBS® game.

When the READER then reads the completed MAD LIBS® game to the other players, they will discover that they have written a story that is fantastic, screamingly funny, shocking, silly, crazy, or just plain dumb—depending upon which words each WRITER called out.

● EXAMPLE (*Before and After*)

"_____!" he said _____
        EXCLAMATION   ADVERB

as he jumped into his convertible _____ and
                                          NOUN

drove off with his _____ wife.
                        ADJECTIVE

"_____Ouch_____!" he said _____stupidly_____
        EXCLAMATION   ADVERB

as he jumped into his convertible _____cat_____ and
                                          NOUN

drove off with his _____brave_____ wife.
                        ADJECTIVE

QUICK REVIEW

In case you have forgotten what adjectives, adverbs, nouns, and verbs are, here is a quick review:

An ADJECTIVE describes something or somebody. *Lumpy, soft, ugly, messy,* and *short* are adjectives.

An ADVERB tells how something is done. It modifies a verb and usually ends in "ly." *Modestly, stupidly, greedily,* and *carefully* are adverbs.

A NOUN is the name of a person, place, or thing. *Sidewalk, umbrella, bridle, bathtub,* and *nose* are nouns.

A VERB is an action word. *Run, pitch, jump,* and *swim* are verbs. Put the verbs in past tense if the directions say PAST TENSE. *Ran, pitched, jumped,* and *swam* are verbs in the past tense.

When we ask for A PLACE, we mean any sort of place: a country or city *(Spain, Cleveland)* or a room *(bathroom, kitchen).*

An EXCLAMATION or SILLY WORD is any sort of funny sound, gasp, grunt, or outcry, like *Wow!, Ouch!, Whomp!, Ick!,* and *Gadzooks!*

When we ask for specific words, like a NUMBER, a COLOR, an ANIMAL, or a PART OF THE BODY, we mean a word that is one of those things, like *seven, blue, horse,* or *head.*

When we ask for a PLURAL, it means more than one. For example, *cat* pluralized is *cats.*

MAD LIBS® is fun to play with friends, but you can also play it by yourself! To begin with, DO NOT look at the story on the page below. Fill in the blanks on this page with the words called for. Then, using the words you have selected, fill in the blank spaces in the story.

Now you've created your own hilarious MAD LIBS® game!

INTERVIEW WITH
A ROCK STAR

_____	PLURAL NOUN
_____	PLURAL NOUN
_____	NOUN
_____	COLOR
_____	VERB
_____	ADJECTIVE
_____	NOUN
_____	NOUN
_____	ADJECTIVE
_____	ADJECTIVE
_____	NUMBER
_____	ADJECTIVE
_____	ADJECTIVE
_____	ADJECTIVE
_____	NOUN
_____	VERB

MAD LIBS®
INTERVIEW WITH A ROCK STAR

QUESTION: Whatever made you choose the name "The Psycho

_____" for your group?
　　　PLURAL NOUN

ANSWER: All the other good names like the "Rolling _____,"
　　　　　　　　　　　　　　　　　　　　　PLURAL NOUN

"_____ Jam," and "_____ Floyd" were taken.
　　NOUN　　　　　　　　　　COLOR

QUESTION: You not only _____ songs, but you play many
　　　　　　　　　　　　VERB

_____ instruments, don't you?
　ADJECTIVE

ANSWER: Yes. I play the electric _____, the bass _____,
　　　　　　　　　　　　　　　NOUN　　　　　　　　NOUN

and the _____ keyboard.
　　　ADJECTIVE

QUESTION: You now have a/an _____ song that is number
　　　　　　　　　　　　　　ADJECTIVE

_____ on the _____ charts. What was the inspiration for
　NUMBER　　　　ADJECTIVE

this _____ song?
　　ADJECTIVE

ANSWER: Believe it or not, it was a/an _____ song that my
　　　　　　　　　　　　　　　　ADJECTIVE

mother used to sing to me when it was time for _____, and it
　　　　　　　　　　　　　　　　　　　　　NOUN

never failed to _____ me to sleep.
　　　　　　VERB

HAVE I GOT A GIRAFFE FOR YOU!

PLURAL NOUN _____

PLURAL NOUN _____

PART OF THE BODY _____

NUMBER _____

PLURAL NOUN _____

PART OF THE BODY _____

TYPE OF LIQUID _____

PART OF THE BODY (PLURAL) _____

PART OF THE BODY _____

ADJECTIVE _____

PLURAL NOUN _____

ADJECTIVE _____

ADJECTIVE _____

VERB ENDING IN "ING" _____

NOUN _____

PLURAL NOUN _____

NOUN _____

MAD LIBS®
HAVE I GOT
A GIRAFFE FOR YOU!

Giraffes have aroused the curiosity of _____ since earliest times.
                                        PLURAL NOUN

The giraffe is the tallest of all living _____, but scientists are
                                          PLURAL NOUN

unable to explain how it got its long _____. The giraffe's
                                        PART OF THE BODY

tremendous height, which might reach _____ _____,
                                        NUMBER   PLURAL NOUN

comes mostly from its legs and _____. If a giraffe wants to
                                 PART OF THE BODY

take a drink of _____ from the ground, it has to spread its
                 TYPE OF LIQUID

_____ far apart in order to reach down and lap up the
PART OF THE BODY (PLURAL)

water with its huge _____. The giraffe has _____
                     PART OF THE BODY   ADJECTIVE

ears that are sensitive to the faintest _____, and it has a/an
                                          PLURAL NOUN

_____ sense of smell and sight. When attacked, a giraffe can put
 ADJECTIVE

up a/an _____ fight by _____ out with its hind
          ADJECTIVE   VERB ENDING IN "ING"

legs and using its head like a sledge _____. Finally, a giraffe can
                                         NOUN

gallop at more than thirty _____ an hour when pursued and can
                            PLURAL NOUN

outrun the fastest _____.
                     NOUN

MAD LIBS® is fun to play with friends, but you can also play it by yourself! To begin with, DO NOT look at the story on the page below. Fill in the blanks on this page with the words called for. Then, using the words you have selected, fill in the blank spaces in the story.

Now you've created your own hilarious MAD LIBS® game!

THE OLYMPICS

NOUN _____

PLURAL NOUN _____

ADJECTIVE _____

PLURAL NOUN _____

PLURAL NOUN _____

NUMBER _____

ADJECTIVE _____

ADJECTIVE _____

NOUN _____

ADJECTIVE _____

VERB ENDING IN "S" _____

PART OF THE BODY _____

NOUN _____

ADJECTIVE _____

PLURAL NOUN _____

PLURAL NOUN _____

MAD LIBS

THE OLYMPICS

Every two years, countries from all over the _____ send their best
                                                    NOUN

_____ to compete in _____ games and win _____.
PLURAL NOUN   ADJECTIVE   PLURAL NOUN

These events are called the Olympic _____, and they started
                                          PLURAL NOUN

_____ years ago in _____ Greece. When a winner
   NUMBER   ADJECTIVE

receives his or her _____ medal at the games, the national
                          ADJECTIVE

_____ of his or her country is played by a/an _____
   NOUN   ADJECTIVE

band. As the band _____, the citizens of that country put
                     VERB ENDING IN "S"

their _____ to their chest and join in the singing of their
         PART OF THE BODY

national _____. Thanks to television, these _____ events
            NOUN   ADJECTIVE

can now be watched by over a billion _____ throughout the world
                                          PLURAL NOUN

every two _____.
             PLURAL NOUN

MAD LIBS® is fun to play with friends, but you can also play it by yourself! To begin with, DO NOT look at the story on the page below. Fill in the blanks on this page with the words called for. Then, using the words you have selected, fill in the blank spaces in the story.

Now you've created your own hilarious MAD LIBS® game!

HOME SWEET HOME

NOUN _____

PART OF THE BODY _____

NUMBER _____

NOUN _____

COLOR _____

ADJECTIVE _____

NOUN _____

NOUN _____

PLURAL NOUN _____

NOUN _____

NOUN _____

ADJECTIVE _____

NOUN _____

ADVERB _____

PART OF THE BODY _____

VERB ENDING IN "ING" _____

ADJECTIVE _____

MAD LIBS

HOME SWEET HOME

Some people are fond of the saying, "Home is where you hang your

_____." Others say, "Home is where the _____
        NOUN   PART OF THE BODY

is." As for me, even though my home is a rustic, _____-story
                                                        NUMBER

_____ home with a/an _____ picket fence surrounding
        NOUN   COLOR

it, I think of it as my _____ castle. Perched on a/an
                                ADJECTIVE

_____ overlooking a babbling _____ and surrounded by
        NOUN   NOUN

a forest of huge _____, my home offers me _____ and
                    PLURAL NOUN   NOUN

tranquility. Each and every _____ I look forward to coming back
                                NOUN

to my _____ home, where my faithful _____ will
            ADJECTIVE   NOUN

_____ greet me by wagging its _____ and
        ADVERB   PART OF THE BODY

_____ all over me. I just love my home _____ home.
VERB ENDING IN "ING"   ADJECTIVE

From GRAB BAG MAD LIBS® • Copyright © 1996, 2001 by Penguin Random House LLC.

MAD LIBS® is fun to play with friends, but you can also play it by yourself! To begin with, DO NOT look at the story on the page below. Fill in the blanks on this page with the words called for. Then, using the words you have selected, fill in the blank spaces in the story.

Now you've created your own hilarious MAD LIBS® game!

INTERVIEW WITH
A COMEDIAN

NOUN _____

ADJECTIVE _____

ADJECTIVE _____

NOUN _____

NUMBER _____

PLURAL NOUN _____

NOUN _____

VERB _____

VERB _____

PLURAL NOUN _____

PLURAL NOUN _____

ADJECTIVE _____

NOUN _____

MAD LIBS®
INTERVIEW WITH
A COMEDIAN

QUESTION: Were you always a stand-up _____ ?
NOUN

ANSWER: No. I had many _____ jobs in my _____
ADJECTIVE   ADJECTIVE

lifetime. I started out as a used _____ salesperson, and then for
NOUN

_____ years, I sold ladies' _____.
NUMBER   PLURAL NOUN

QUESTION: When did you discover you were a funny _____
NOUN

who could make people _____ out loud?
VERB

ANSWER: It was in school. The first time our teacher had us do show and

_____, I made the _____ in my class laugh so hard
VERB   PLURAL NOUN

they fell out of their _____.
PLURAL NOUN

QUESTION: How would you describe your _____ act?
ADJECTIVE

ANSWER: I am a thinking person's _____.
NOUN

MOVIES SHOULD BE FUN

PLURAL NOUN _____

ADJECTIVE _____

PLURAL NOUN _____

NOUN _____

ADJECTIVE _____

NOUN _____

NOUN _____

PERSON IN ROOM (MALE) _____

A PLACE _____

ADJECTIVE _____

PERSON IN ROOM _____

PERSON IN ROOM _____

ADJECTIVE _____

PLURAL NOUN _____

PART OF THE BODY (PLURAL) _____

MAD LIBS® is fun to play with friends, but you can also play it by yourself! To begin with, DO NOT look at the story on the page below. Fill in the blanks on this page with the words called for. Then, using the words you have selected, fill in the blank spaces in the story.

Now you've created your own hilarious MAD LIBS® game!

MAD LIBS®

MOVIES SHOULD BE FUN

In recent years, there have been too many disaster movies in which tall

_____ catch on fire, _____ dinosaurs come to life, and
PLURAL NOUN   ADJECTIVE

huge _____ attack people in the ocean, making you afraid to get
PLURAL NOUN

out of your _____ in the morning. Movie fans ask why we can't
NOUN

have more _____ pictures like *It's a Wonderful* _____,
ADJECTIVE   NOUN

Gone with the _____, or *Mr.* _____ *Goes to (the)*
NOUN   PERSON IN ROOM (MALE)

_____. These films made you feel _____ all over.
A PLACE   ADJECTIVE

These same fans also ask why we can't have more funny films with comedians

such as Laurel and _____, and Abbott and _____.
PERSON IN ROOM   PERSON IN ROOM

These _____ performers gave us great slapstick _____
ADJECTIVE   PLURAL NOUN

that still makes our _____ ache from laughing.
PART OF THE BODY (PLURAL)

COOL IT

PLURAL NOUN _____

ADJECTIVE _____

NOUN _____

ADJECTIVE _____

NOUN _____

NOUN _____

NOUN _____

NOUN _____

ADJECTIVE _____

VERB ENDING IN "ING" _____

NOUN _____

ADJECTIVE _____

NOUN _____

VERB _____

MAD LIBS® is fun to play with friends, but you can also play it by yourself! To begin with, DO NOT look at the story on the page below. Fill in the blanks on this page with the words called for. Then, using the words you have selected, fill in the blank spaces in the story.

Now you've created your own hilarious MAD LIBS® game!

MAD LIBS

COOL IT

Weather plays an important part in our daily _____. What is
_____ PLURAL NOUN

weather, anyway? According to _____ scientists, who are known
_____ ADJECTIVE

as meteorologists, weather is what the air is like at any time of the

_____. It doesn't matter if the air is cold, hot, or _____,
NOUN ADJECTIVE

it's all weather. Weather changes from hour to _____, from day to
NOUN

_____, from season to _____, and from year to
NOUN NOUN

_____. Daily changes in weather are caused by _____
NOUN ADJECTIVE

storms _____ across the earth. Seasonal changes are from the
VERB ENDING IN "ING"

earth moving around the _____. When the vapors in _____
NOUN ADJECTIVE

clouds condense, we have _____ and snow. Whether you like it or
NOUN

not, weather is here to _____.
VERB

GOING TO TOWN

LAST NAME _____

ADJECTIVE _____

PLURAL NOUN _____

ADJECTIVE _____

PERSON IN ROOM _____

PLURAL NOUN _____

PLURAL NOUN _____

ADJECTIVE _____

NOUN _____

NUMBER _____

VERB ENDING IN "ING" _____

ADJECTIVE _____

ADJECTIVE _____

ADJECTIVE _____

NOUN _____

NOUN _____

MAD LIBS® is fun to play with friends, but you can also play it by yourself! To begin with, DO NOT look at the story on the page below. Fill in the blanks on this page with the words called for. Then, using the words you have selected, fill in the blank spaces in the story.

MAD LIBS®

GOING TO TOWN

THE ART SCENE

Today the _____ Gallery presents a series of _____
          LAST NAME   ADJECTIVE

landscape paintings and still-life _____ by the _____
                                      PLURAL NOUN   ADJECTIVE

artist, _____. These beautiful _____ will be on
         PERSON IN ROOM   PLURAL NOUN

exhibition for the next three _____.
                                 PLURAL NOUN

MUSIC

Tonight marks the _____ debut of the all-_____ choir
                    ADJECTIVE   NOUN

of _____ great _____ voices. This _____
     NUMBER   VERB ENDING IN "ING"   ADJECTIVE

ensemble will present _____ renditions of such _____
                        ADJECTIVE   ADJECTIVE

children's songs as "Twinkle Twinkle Little _____" and "Old
                                               NOUN

MacDonald Had a/an _____."
                     NOUN

From GRAB BAG MAD LIBS® • Copyright © 1996, 2001 by Penguin Random House LLC.

MAD LIBS® is fun to play with friends, but you can also play it by yourself! To begin with, DO NOT look at the story on the page below. Fill in the blanks on this page with the words called for. Then, using the words you have selected, fill in the blank spaces in the story.

Now you've created your own hilarious MAD LIBS® game!

THE THREE MUSKETEERS

ADJECTIVE _____

PLURAL NOUN _____

ADJECTIVE _____

NOUN _____

ADJECTIVE _____

NOUN _____

NOUN _____

PLURAL NOUN _____

NOUN _____

PERSON IN ROOM _____

PLURAL NOUN _____

ADJECTIVE _____

NOUN _____

NOUN _____

PLURAL NOUN _____

NOUN _____

MAD LIBS

THE THREE MUSKETEERS

There is no more rousing story in _____ literature than *The*
ADJECTIVE

Three _____. This _____ romance by the great French
PLURAL NOUN ADJECTIVE

_____ Alexander Dumas, tells the story of D' Artagnan, a/an
NOUN

_____ young _____ who arrives in 17th-century Paris
ADJECTIVE NOUN

riding a/an _____ with only three _____ in his pocket.
NOUN PLURAL NOUN

Determined to be in the service of the _____ who rules all of
NOUN

France, he duels with Athos, Pathos, and _____, three of the
PERSON IN ROOM

king's best _____. Eventually, these swordsmen and D' Artagnan
PLURAL NOUN

save their _____ king from being overthrown and losing his
ADJECTIVE

_____. Over the years, *The Three Musketeers* has been made into a
NOUN

stage _____, two motion _____, and, most recently,
NOUN PLURAL NOUN

into a Broadway _____.
NOUN

SNOW WHITE

PLURAL NOUN _____

PLURAL NOUN _____

ADJECTIVE _____

PLURAL NOUN _____

ADJECTIVE _____

NOUN _____

NOUN _____

ADJECTIVE _____

ADJECTIVE _____

PLURAL NOUN _____

NOUN _____

COLOR _____

NOUN _____

PART OF THE BODY _____

ADVERB _____

MAD LIBS® is fun to play with friends, but you can also play it by yourself! To begin with, DO NOT look at the story on the page below. Fill in the blanks on this page with the words called for. Then, using the words you have selected, fill in the blank spaces in the story.

Now you've created your own hilarious MAD LIBS® game!

MAD LIBS

SNOW WHITE

One of the most popular fairy _____ of all time is *Snow White*
                                PLURAL NOUN

and the Seven _____. Snow White is a princess whose _____
              PLURAL NOUN   ADJECTIVE

beauty threatens her stepmother, the queen, and her two step-_____,
                                                              PLURAL NOUN

who are very _____. Snow White is forced to flee from the
             ADJECTIVE

_____ in which she lives and hide in the nearby _____.
   NOUN   NOUN

Once there, she is discovered by _____ animals who guide her to
                                  ADJECTIVE

the _____ cottage of the seven dwarfs. The dwarfs come home
     ADJECTIVE

from digging in their mine and discover Snow White asleep in their

_____. The dwarfs take care of her until a prince, who has traveled
PLURAL NOUN

the four corners of the _____ in search of Snow _____,
                          NOUN   COLOR

arrives and gives her a magical _____ on her _____,
                                  NOUN   PART OF THE BODY

which miraculously brings her back to life. Snow White and the prince live

_____ ever after.
   ADVERB

MAD LIBS® is fun to play with friends, but you can also play it by yourself! To begin with, DO NOT look at the story on the page below. Fill in the blanks on this page with the words called for. Then, using the words you have selected, fill in the blank spaces in the story.

Now you've created your own hilarious MAD LIBS® game!

MAGIC, ANYONE?

PLURAL NOUN _____

ADJECTIVE _____

ADJECTIVE _____

NOUN _____

NOUN _____

NOUN _____

NOUN _____

ADJECTIVE _____

PART OF THE BODY _____

PLURAL NOUN _____

ADJECTIVE _____

NOUN _____

ADJECTIVE _____

NOUN _____

PART OF THE BODY (PLURAL) _____

PART OF THE BODY _____

PLURAL NOUN _____

MAD LIBS®

MAGIC, ANYONE?

_____ of all ages enjoy watching _____ magicians
   PLURAL NOUN   ADJECTIVE

perform their _____ tricks. Every man, woman, and _____
             ADJECTIVE   NOUN

loves to see a magician pull a/an _____ out of a hat, saw a live
                                 NOUN

_____ in half, or make a huge _____ disappear into
  NOUN   NOUN

_____ air. Audiences love when magicians perform sleight of
  ADJECTIVE

_____ with a deck of _____, a/an _____
 PART OF THE BODY   PLURAL NOUN   ADJECTIVE

coin, or a silk _____. The greatest of all magicians was the
           NOUN

_____ Harry Houdini, who was able to escape from a locked
  ADJECTIVE

_____ even though his _____ were tied
  NOUN   PART OF THE BODY (PLURAL)

behind his _____ and his feet were wrapped in iron _____.
   PART OF THE BODY   PLURAL NOUN

MAD LIBS® is fun to play with friends, but you can also play it by yourself! To begin with, DO NOT look at the story on the page below. Fill in the blanks on this page with the words called for. Then, using the words you have selected, fill in the blank spaces in the story.

Now you've created your own hilarious MAD LIBS® game!

THE BIG GAME

PLURAL NOUN _____

PERSON IN ROOM _____

NOUN _____

LAST NAME _____

PLURAL NOUN _____

A PLACE _____

PLURAL NOUN _____

A PLACE _____

PLURAL NOUN _____

NOUN _____

ADJECTIVE _____

ADJECTIVE _____

NOUN _____

NOUN _____

NOUN _____

VERB _____

ADJECTIVE _____

THE BIG GAME

To be read with great enthusiasm!

Hello there, sports _____! This is _____, talking to
                        PLURAL NOUN   PERSON IN ROOM

you from the press _____ in _____ Stadium, where
                        NOUN   LAST NAME

57,000 cheering _____ have gathered to watch (the) _____
                    PLURAL NOUN   A PLACE

_____ take on (the) _____ _____. Even
  PLURAL NOUN   A PLACE   PLURAL NOUN

though the _____ is shining, it's a/an _____ cold day
                NOUN   ADJECTIVE

with the temperature in the _____ 20s. A strong _____
                                ADJECTIVE   NOUN

is blowing fiercely across the playing _____ that will definitely
                                            NOUN

affect the passing _____. We'll be back for the opening
                          NOUN

_____-off after a few words from our _____ sponsor.
    VERB   ADJECTIVE

THINGS TO DO THIS WEEKEND

_____ LAST NAME

_____ ADJECTIVE

_____ PLURAL NOUN

_____ PLURAL NOUN

_____ NOUN

_____ ADJECTIVE

_____ NOUN

_____ ADVERB

_____ NOUN

_____ ADJECTIVE

_____ PLURAL NOUN

_____ PERSON IN ROOM

_____ ADJECTIVE

_____ NOUN

_____ ADJECTIVE

_____ ADJECTIVE

_____ NOUN

_____ NOUN

_____ ADJECTIVE

MAD LIBS®
THINGS TO DO
THIS WEEKEND

FILM

_____ Theaters offers a/an _____ program of foreign
　LAST NAME　　　　　　　　　　　　　　ADJECTIVE

_____ never before seen in American _____ . The first
　PLURAL NOUN　　　　　　　　　　　　　　　　　　　PLURAL NOUN

film to be shown will be *Henry and the* _____ . This is the
　　　　　　　　　　　　　　　　　　　　　　　　NOUN

_____ love story of a man and his _____ . It will be
　ADJECTIVE　　　　　　　　　　　　　　　　　　NOUN

shown _____ until the end of the _____ .
　　　　ADVERB　　　　　　　　　　　　　　　　NOUN

STAGE

Appearing in our _____ theater for the next three _____
　　　　　　　　　　　ADJECTIVE　　　　　　　　　　　　　　　　　PLURAL NOUN

is _____ , that very _____ star of stage, screen, and
　PERSON IN ROOM　　　　　　　ADJECTIVE

_____ . He/she will be appearing with our _____
　NOUN　　　　　　　　　　　　　　　　　　　　　　　　　　　　ADJECTIVE

repertory company in nightly performances of William Shakespeare's

_____ comedy, *A Midsummer Night's* _____ . Tickets
　ADJECTIVE　　　　　　　　　　　　　　　　　　　　　　　NOUN

can be purchased now at the _____ office by telephone, fax, or
　　　　　　　　　　　　　　　　　　NOUN

_____ card.
　ADJECTIVE

SCENE FROM A HORROR PICTURE

_____ ADJECTIVE

_____ PART OF THE BODY

_____ PLURAL NOUN

_____ NOUN

_____ ADJECTIVE

_____ PLURAL NOUN

_____ EXCLAMATION

_____ NOUN

_____ PART OF THE BODY

_____ PERSON IN ROOM

_____ NOUN

_____ PART OF THE BODY

_____ ADJECTIVE

_____ VERB

_____ ADVERB

_____ NOUN

_____ NOUN

MAD LIBS®
SCENE FROM A
HORROR PICTURE

To be read aloud (preferably by live people):

Actor #1: Why did we have to come to this _____ old castle? This
                                              ADJECTIVE

place sends shivers up and down my _____.
                                     PART OF THE BODY

Actor #2: We had no choice. You know all the _____ in town were
                                               PLURAL NOUN

filled because of the _____ convention.
                        NOUN

Actor #1: I'd have been happy to stay in a/an _____ motel.
                                                ADJECTIVE

Actor #2: Relax. Here comes the bellboy for our _____.
                                                  PLURAL NOUN

Actor #1: _____! Look, he's all bent over and has a big
            EXCLAMATION

_____ riding on his _____. He looks just like
   NOUN   PART OF THE BODY

_____ from that horror flick, *Frankenstein.*
 PERSON IN ROOM

Actor #2: No. I think he's my old _____ teacher.
                                    NOUN

Actor #1: I'm putting my _____ down! I'm not staying in this
                           PART OF THE BODY

_____ place. I'd rather _____ in the car!
 ADJECTIVE   VERB

Actor #2: You're worrying _____.
                            ADVERB

Actor #1: Really? Look at the bellboy. He has my _____ in one hand,
                                                   NOUN

your _____ in the other, and his third hand . . . His *third* hand?
       NOUN

Ahhhhh!

IN THE GOOD OLD SUMMERTIME

PLURAL NOUN _____

PLURAL NOUN _____

ADVERB _____

VERB ENDING IN "ING" _____

ADJECTIVE _____

NUMBER _____

PART OF THE BODY _____

PLURAL NOUN _____

NOUN _____

PLURAL NOUN _____

TYPE OF LIQUID _____

NOUN _____

ADVERB _____

PLURAL NOUN _____

PLURAL NOUN _____

NOUN _____

NOUN _____

NOUN _____

NOUN _____

MAD LIBS® is fun to play with friends, but you can also play it by yourself! To begin with, DO NOT look at the story on the page below. Fill in the blanks on this page with the words called for. Then, using the words you have selected, fill in the blank spaces in the story.

Now you've created your own hilarious MAD LIBS® game!

MAD LIBS®
IN THE GOOD OLD SUMMERTIME

Many selective _____ prefer the Summer Olympics to the Winter
                    PLURAL NOUN

_____. They respond _____ to such swimming and
   PLURAL NOUN   ADVERB

_____ competitions as the hundred-meter _____
VERB ENDING IN "ING"   ADJECTIVE

-style race, the _____-meter _____-stroke race, and, of
                    NUMBER   PART OF THE BODY

course, the diving contests in which _____ dive off a high
                                          PLURAL NOUN

_____ and do triple _____ in the air before landing in
     NOUN   PLURAL NOUN

the _____. Equally fascinating are the track and _____
     TYPE OF LIQUID   NOUN

events in which _____ conditioned _____ compete for
                     ADVERB   PLURAL NOUN

gold _____. They compete in such exciting events as the 1,500-
       PLURAL NOUN

_____ race, the hundred-_____ dash, the ever-popular
     NOUN   NOUN

_____ vaulting, and, last but not least, throwing the hammer, the
     NOUN

javelin, and the _____.
                      NOUN

GOOD MANNERS

NOUN _____

NOUN _____

NOUN _____

VERB _____

PART OF THE BODY _____

ADVERB _____

NOUN _____

NOUN _____

NOUN _____

NOUN _____

PART OF THE BODY (PLURAL) _____

NOUN _____

ADJECTIVE _____

ADVERB _____

MAD LIBS® is fun to play with friends, but you can also play it by yourself! To begin with, DO NOT look at the story on the page below. Fill in the blanks on this page with the words called for. Then, using the words you have selected, fill in the blank spaces in the story.

Now you've created your own hilarious MAD LIBS® game!

MAD LIBS®

GOOD MANNERS

1. When you receive a birthday _____ or a wedding _____,
   NOUN   NOUN

   you should always send a thank-you _____.
                                        NOUN

2. When you _____ or burp out loud, be sure to cover your
              VERB

   _____ and say, "I'm _____ sorry."
   PART OF THE BODY   ADVERB

3. If you are a man and wearing a/an _____ on your head and a/an
                                        NOUN

   _____ approaches, it's always polite to tip your _____.
   NOUN   NOUN

4. When you are at a friend's _____ for dinner, remember, it's not
                                NOUN

   polite to eat with your _____, take food from
                            PART OF THE BODY (PLURAL)

   anyone else's _____, or leave the table before everyone else.
                  NOUN

5. When meeting your friend's parents, always try to make a/an _____
                                                               ADJECTIVE

   impression by greeting them _____.
                               ADVERB

MAD LIBS® is fun to play with friends, but you can also play it by yourself! To begin with, DO NOT look at the story on the page below. Fill in the blanks on this page with the words called for. Then, using the words you have selected, fill in the blank spaces in the story.

Now you've created your own hilarious MAD LIBS® game!

TV GUIDANCE
PICK OF THE WEEK

_____ NOUN

_____ ADJECTIVE

_____ NUMBER

_____ PLURAL NOUN

_____ PLURAL NOUN

_____ NOUN

_____ PART OF THE BODY (PLURAL)

_____ ADJECTIVE

_____ PERSON IN ROOM (FEMALE)

_____ NOUN

_____ PART OF THE BODY

_____ PLURAL NOUN

_____ ADJECTIVE

_____ ADJECTIVE

_____ PERSON IN ROOM

_____ NOUN

_____ NOUN

MAD LIBS®
TV GUIDANCE
PICK OF THE WEEK

THURSDAY, 8:00 P.M. *My Adventures as a Foreign* _____.
                                                      NOUN

This is an exciting and _____ made-for-TV movie that takes
                          ADJECTIVE

place during the time of World War _____. We give it a rating of
                                    NUMBER

three _____.
       PLURAL NOUN

FRIDAY, 7:30 P.M. *Happy* _____.
                          PLURAL NOUN

When an old high-school _____ welcomes him with open
                          NOUN

_____ and throws him a/an _____ party, this
PART OF THE BODY (PLURAL)   ADJECTIVE

puts _____, his former _____ friend, into a bad
      PERSON IN ROOM (FEMALE)   NOUN

state of _____.
          PART OF THE BODY

SATURDAY, 10:00 P.M. *Where Have All the* _____ *Gone?* This
                                           PLURAL NOUN

_____ thriller, by the _____ director
ADJECTIVE   ADJECTIVE

_____, is about a Manhattan _____ searching for a
PERSON IN ROOM   NOUN

missing person in a small _____.
                           NOUN

MAD LIBS® is fun to play with friends, but you can also play it by yourself! To begin with, DO NOT look at the story on the page below. Fill in the blanks on this page with the words called for. Then, using the words you have selected, fill in the blank spaces in the story.

Now you've created your own hilarious MAD LIBS® game!

GOOD HEALTH TO ONE AND ALL

_____
ADJECTIVE

_____
ADJECTIVE

_____
VERB ENDING IN "ING"

_____
PART OF THE BODY (PLURAL)

_____
PLURAL NOUN

_____
PLURAL NOUN

_____
NOUN

_____
PLURAL NOUN

_____
PLURAL NOUN

_____
NOUN

_____
PLURAL NOUN

_____
PLURAL NOUN

_____
ADJECTIVE

_____
PLURAL NOUN

_____
ADJECTIVE

_____
ADJECTIVE

MAD LIBS®
GOOD HEALTH
TO ONE AND ALL

A/An _____ fitness revolution is taking place. Today, millions of
        ADJECTIVE

people are doing all kinds of _____ exercises such as jogging,
                                    ADJECTIVE

walking, and _____ to get their _____
              VERB ENDING IN "ING"   PART OF THE BODY (PLURAL)

in shape and develop their _____. Many go to gyms and health
                              PLURAL NOUN

_____ to work out by punching a/an _____, lifting
   PLURAL NOUN   NOUN

_____, or performing aerobic _____. In the past
   PLURAL NOUN   PLURAL NOUN

_____ people have become very weight conscious. They have
   NOUN

learned what _____ they should and should not eat. They know it's
              PLURAL NOUN

healthy to eat green _____ and _____ fruit. They also
                      PLURAL NOUN   ADJECTIVE

know to avoid foods high in _____ and _____ fats,
                              PLURAL NOUN   ADJECTIVE

especially if they want to lead a long and _____ life.
                                              ADJECTIVE

MAD LIBS® is fun to play with friends, but you can also play it by yourself! To begin with, DO NOT look at the story on the page below. Fill in the blanks on this page with the words called for. Then, using the words you have selected, fill in the blank spaces in the story.

Now you've created your own hilarious MAD LIBS® game!

WHY DO SKUNKS SMELL?

NOUN _____

ADJECTIVE _____

PLURAL NOUN _____

A PLACE _____

PLURAL NOUN _____

ADJECTIVE _____

NOUN _____

VERB ENDING IN "ING" _____

PART OF THE BODY _____

PART OF THE BODY (PLURAL) _____

PART OF THE BODY (PLURAL) _____

ADVERB _____

COLOR _____

PART OF THE BODY _____

PART OF THE BODY _____

MAD LIBS

WHY DO SKUNKS SMELL?

Surprisingly, a skunk is a friendly _____ who can make a/an
                                        NOUN

_____ household pet. But what makes these _____
    ADJECTIVE   PLURAL NOUN

smell to high (the) _____? The skunk has scent _____
                        A PLACE   PLURAL NOUN

that contain a/an _____-smelling fluid. When attacked, the
                      ADJECTIVE

skunk aims this smelly _____ at its enemies. But the skunk does
                            NOUN

give warning before _____. It raises its _____
                      VERB ENDING IN "ING"   PART OF THE BODY

first, or stamps its _____ so that you can run away as fast
                      PART OF THE BODY (PLURAL)

as your _____ can carry you. The most _____
          PART OF THE BODY (PLURAL)   ADVERB

recognizable skunk is the one with a _____ line on its _____
                                          COLOR   PART OF THE BODY

and another one between its _____ and its ears.
                                PART OF THE BODY

MAD LIBS® is fun to play with friends, but you can also play it by yourself! To begin with, DO NOT look at the story on the page below. Fill in the blanks on this page with the words called for. Then, using the words you have selected, fill in the blank spaces in the story.

Now you've created your own hilarious MAD LIBS® game!

FAMOUS QUOTES FROM THE AMERICAN REVOLUTION

NOUN _____

NOUN _____

COLOR _____

PART OF THE BODY (PLURAL) _____

NOUN _____

PLURAL NOUN _____

VERB ENDING IN "ING" _____

NOUN _____

PLURAL NOUN _____

PLURAL NOUN _____

ADJECTIVE _____

NOUN _____

MAD LIBS®
FAMOUS QUOTES FROM
THE AMERICAN REVOLUTION

Nathan Hale said: "I regret that I have but one _____ to give for

NOUN

my _____."

NOUN

William Prescott said: "Don't fire until you see the _____ of their

COLOR

_____."

PART OF THE BODY (PLURAL)

Patrick Henry said: "Give me liberty or give me _____."

NOUN

Paul Revere said: "The _____ are _____."

PLURAL NOUN   VERB ENDING IN "ING"

John Hancock said: "I wrote my _____ large so the king could

NOUN

read it without his _____."

PLURAL NOUN

Thomas Jefferson said: "All _____ are created equal. They are

PLURAL NOUN

endowed by their creator with certain _____ rights and among

ADJECTIVE

these are life, liberty, and the pursuit of _____."

NOUN

MAD LIBS®

SLEEPOVER PARTY
MAD LIBS

by Roger Price and Leonard Stern

MAD LIBS®

INSTRUCTIONS

MAD LIBS® is a game for people who don't like games!
It can be played by one, two, three, four, or forty.

• RIDICULOUSLY SIMPLE DIRECTIONS

In this tablet you will find stories containing blank spaces where words are left out. One player, the READER, selects one of these stories. The READER does not tell anyone what the story is about. Instead, he/she asks the other players, the WRITERS, to give him/her words. These words are used to fill in the blank spaces in the story.

• TO PLAY

The READER asks each WRITER in turn to call out a word—an adjective or a noun or whatever the space calls for—and uses them to fill in the blank spaces in the story. The result is a MAD LIBS® game.

When the READER then reads the completed MAD LIBS® game to the other players, they will discover that they have written a story that is fantastic, screamingly funny, shocking, silly, crazy, or just plain dumb—depending upon which words each WRITER called out.

• EXAMPLE (*Before* and *After*)

"_____!" he said _____
      EXCLAMATION   ADVERB

as he jumped into his convertible _____ and
                                             NOUN

drove off with his _____ wife.
                     ADJECTIVE

"*Ouch*!" he said *stupidly*
      EXCLAMATION   ADVERB

as he jumped into his convertible *cat* and
                                             NOUN

drove off with his *brave* wife.
                     ADJECTIVE

MAD LIBS®

QUICK REVIEW

In case you have forgotten what adjectives, adverbs, nouns, and verbs are, here is a quick review:

An ADJECTIVE describes something or somebody. *Lumpy, soft, ugly, messy,* and *short* are adjectives.

An ADVERB tells how something is done. It modifies a verb and usually ends in "ly." *Modestly, stupidly, greedily,* and *carefully* are adverbs.

A NOUN is the name of a person, place, or thing. *Sidewalk, umbrella, bridle, bathtub,* and *nose* are nouns.

A VERB is an action word. *Run, pitch, jump,* and *swim* are verbs. Put the verbs in past tense if the directions say PAST TENSE. *Ran, pitched, jumped,* and *swam* are verbs in the past tense.

When we ask for A PLACE, we mean any sort of place: a country or city *(Spain, Cleveland)* or a room *(bathroom, kitchen).*

An EXCLAMATION or SILLY WORD is any sort of funny sound, gasp, grunt, or outcry, like *Wow!, Ouch!, Whomp!, Ick!,* and *Gadzooks!*

When we ask for specific words, like a NUMBER, a COLOR, an ANIMAL, or a PART OF THE BODY, we mean a word that is one of those things, like *seven, blue, horse,* or *head.*

When we ask for a PLURAL, it means more than one. For example, *cat* pluralized is *cats.*

MAD LIBS® is fun to play with friends, but you can also play it by yourself! To begin with, DO NOT look at the story on the page below. Fill in the blanks on this page with the words called for. Then, using the words you have selected, fill in the blank spaces in the story.

Now you've created your own hilarious MAD LIBS® game!

YOU'RE INVITED

_____ PERSON IN ROOM (FEMALE)

_____ ADJECTIVE

_____ NOUN

_____ NOUN

_____ CELEBRITY

_____ ADVERB

_____ NUMBER

_____ ADJECTIVE

_____ NOUN

_____ NOUN

_____ PART OF THE BODY

_____ PLURAL NOUN

_____ ADJECTIVE

_____ PLURAL NOUN

_____ PLURAL NOUN

_____ ADJECTIVE

_____ PLURAL NOUN

_____ LETTER OF THE ALPHABET

_____ CELEBRITY

_____ SAME CELEBRITY

_____ ADJECTIVE

MAD LIBS®

YOU'RE INVITED

Dear _____,
PERSON IN ROOM (FEMALE)

I would like to invite you to a/an _____ sleepover party this Friday
ADJECTIVE

night at my _____. I live on the corner of South _____ Street
NOUN   NOUN

and _____ Lane. Please arrive _____ at _____ o'clock.
CELEBRITY   ADVERB   NUMBER

Don't forget to bring a/an _____ sleeping _____ and a
ADJECTIVE   NOUN

soft _____ to rest your _____ on. We'll have pizza
NOUN   PART OF THE BODY

topped with _____ for dinner, and we'll watch a/an
PLURAL NOUN

_____ movie. When it is time for bed, we'll all change into our
ADJECTIVE

_____ and turn out the _____. Then we'll tell
PLURAL NOUN   PLURAL NOUN

_____ ghost stories and talk about all the cute _____ at
ADJECTIVE   PLURAL NOUN

school! Please RSV-_____ to me by e-mail at iluv-
LETTER OF THE ALPHABET

_____@_____.com. Hope you can join our _____
CELEBRITY   SAME CELEBRITY   ADJECTIVE

party!

From SLEEPOVER PARTY MAD LIBS® • Copyright © 2008 by Penguin Random House LLC.

LET'S GET PACKING!

NOUN _____

ADJECTIVE _____

NOUN _____

ADJECTIVE _____

PLURAL NOUN _____

NOUN _____

PART OF THE BODY (PLURAL) _____

VERB _____

ADJECTIVE _____

CELEBRITY _____

VERB _____

ADVERB _____

ADJECTIVE _____

NOUN _____

VERB _____

VERB ENDING IN "ING" _____

NOUN _____

ADJECTIVE _____

MAD LIBS® is fun to play with friends, but you can also play it by yourself! To begin with, DO NOT look at the story on the page below. Fill in the blanks on this page with the words called for. Then, using the words you have selected, fill in the blank spaces in the story.

Now you've created your own hilarious MAD LIBS® game!

MAD LIBS

LET'S GET PACKING!

If you are going to a sleepover at a friend's _____, here's a/an
                                                    NOUN

_____ list of things to put in your overnight _____:
ADJECTIVE   NOUN

1. _____ pajamas and a change of _____ for the next day.
   ADJECTIVE   PLURAL NOUN

2. A tooth-_____ for brushing your _____.
              NOUN   PART OF THE BODY (PLURAL)

3. Some CDs so you and your friends can _____ to your favorite
                                        VERB

_____ tunes.
ADJECTIVE

4. Magazines with someone like _____ on the cover and articles
                               CELEBRITY

about how to _____ _____.
             VERB   ADVERB

5. A/An _____ _____-light will help you to
        ADJECTIVE   NOUN

_____ in the dark while you stay up _____
VERB   VERB ENDING IN "ING"

into the wee hours of the _____.
                          NOUN

If you follow this checklist, you should have a really _____
                                                       ADJECTIVE

sleepover.

From SLEEPOVER PARTY MAD LIBS® • Copyright © 2008 by Penguin Random House LLC.

MAD LIBS® is fun to play with friends, but you can also play it by yourself! To begin with, DO NOT look at the story on the page below. Fill in the blanks on this page with the words called for. Then, using the words you have selected, fill in the blank spaces in the story.

Now you've created your own hilarious MAD LIBS® game!

PILLOW FIGHT!

ADJECTIVE _____

PERSON IN ROOM (FEMALE) _____

ADJECTIVE _____

NOUN _____

PART OF THE BODY _____

NOUN _____

PERSON IN ROOM (FEMALE) _____

PART OF THE BODY (PLURAL) _____

NOUN _____

PLURAL NOUN _____

ADJECTIVE _____

ADJECTIVE _____

ADJECTIVE _____

MAD LIBS

PILLOW FIGHT!

The last time I went to a sleepover, a/an _____ pillow fight broke
                                              ADJECTIVE

out. Out of nowhere, _____ grabbed her
                         PERSON IN ROOM (FEMALE)

_____, fluffy _____ and began swinging it at anyone
     ADJECTIVE   NOUN

close to her. Soon, everyone else joined in! At one point, I got hit right in the

back of my _____. As soon as I recovered, I tossed my
                PART OF THE BODY

_____ at _____'s _____, but I
     NOUN   PERSON IN ROOM (FEMALE)   PART OF THE BODY (PLURAL)

missed. Instead, I knocked over an expensive _____ and my pillow
                                                    NOUN

split open! _____ flew everywhere, covering the room in a layer of
            PLURAL NOUN

_____ feathers. The fighting stopped when we all broke out in
  ADJECTIVE

_____ laughter. The fun ended when we realized we had to clean up
  ADJECTIVE

the _____ mess!
      ADJECTIVE

From SLEEPOVER PARTY MAD LIBS® • Copyright © 2008 by Penguin Random House LLC.

MAD LIBS' is fun to play with friends, but you can also play it by yourself! To begin with, DO NOT look at the story on the page below. Fill in the blanks on this page with the words called for. Then, using the words you have selected, fill in the blank spaces in the story.

Now you've created your own hilarious MAD LIBS' game!

SLEEPWALKING

VERB ENDING IN "ING" _____

ADJECTIVE _____

PLURAL NOUN _____

PLURAL NOUN _____

VERB _____

PART OF THE BODY (PLURAL) _____

VERB _____

ADJECTIVE _____

NOUN _____

NOUN _____

PLURAL NOUN _____

ADJECTIVE _____

NOUN _____

SILLY WORD _____

PLURAL NOUN _____

Sleep-_____ is a/an _____ phenomenon that a
     VERB ENDING IN "ING"   ADJECTIVE

surprising number of _____ experience. Usually, sleepwalkers climb
             PLURAL NOUN

out of their _____ and begin to _____ with their
       PLURAL NOUN   VERB

_____ tightly shut. Sometimes they _____
PART OF THE BODY (PLURAL)   VERB

outdoors wearing only their _____ pajamas. And it's not
             ADJECTIVE

uncommon for _____-walkers to raid the _____ and eat lots
      NOUN   NOUN

of _____. What's truly amazing is that they don't remember a/an
  PLURAL NOUN

_____ thing the following _____. They'll open the fridge
  ADJECTIVE   NOUN

and say, "_____! Where did all the _____ go?" They may
    SILLY WORD   PLURAL NOUN

never know!

MAD LIBS® is fun to play with friends, but you can also play it by yourself! To begin with, DO NOT look at the story on the page below. Fill in the blanks on this page with the words called for. Then, using the words you have selected, fill in the blank spaces in the story.

Now you've created your own hilarious MAD LIBS® game!

M.A.S.H.

ADJECTIVE _____

NUMBER _____

PLURAL NOUN _____

A PLACE _____

PERSON IN ROOM (MALE) _____

ADJECTIVE _____

A PLACE _____

ADJECTIVE _____

ADJECTIVE _____

NOUN _____

A PLACE _____

ADJECTIVE _____

NUMBER _____

NOUN _____

NUMBER _____

OCCUPATION _____

NOUN _____

ADJECTIVE _____

MAD LIBS

M.A.S.H.

Congratulations! According to M.A.S.H. (the ultimate sleepover game), your

future looks bright and _____. When you are _____ years
                            ADJECTIVE   NUMBER

old, you will meet the man of your _____ at (the)
                                        PLURAL NOUN

_____. His name will be _____. You will have a/an
   A PLACE   PERSON IN ROOM (MALE)

_____ wedding, and you will go to (the) _____ on
   ADJECTIVE   A PLACE

your _____ honeymoon. When you return, you will move into a/an
        ADJECTIVE

_____ _____ in (the) _____. You will drive
   ADJECTIVE   NOUN   A PLACE

a/an _____ car. Then, when you have been married for _____
         ADJECTIVE   NUMBER

years, you will have your first _____. You will go on to have
                                    NOUN

_____ more children. You will work as a/an _____ until you
   NUMBER   OCCUPATION

retire and move to a tropical _____. Your M.A.S.H. future
                                   NOUN

looks prosperous and _____, so prepare to enjoy it!
                         ADJECTIVE

MAD LIBS® is fun to play with friends, but you can also play it by yourself! To begin with, DO NOT look at the story on the page below. Fill in the blanks on this page with the words called for. Then, using the words you have selected, fill in the blank spaces in the story.

Now you've created your own hilarious MAD LIBS® game!

PRANKS FOR NOTHING

ADJECTIVE _____

ADJECTIVE _____

PLURAL NOUN _____

ADJECTIVE _____

PLURAL NOUN _____

PLURAL NOUN _____

ADJECTIVE _____

VERB ENDING IN "ING" _____

NOUN _____

NOUN _____

ADJECTIVE _____

NOUN _____

ADJECTIVE _____

PART OF THE BODY _____

ADJECTIVE _____

PLURAL NOUN _____

PART OF THE BODY (PLURAL) _____

ADJECTIVE _____

PART OF THE BODY (PLURAL) _____

COLOR _____

MAD LIBS

PRANKS FOR NOTHING

Whenever my _____ sister and her _____
               ADJECTIVE   ADJECTIVE

_____ have a sleepover party, I love to play _____ pranks
PLURAL NOUN   ADJECTIVE

on them. Once, I put gummy _____ in everyone's sleeping
                                   PLURAL NOUN

_____. They thought they were _____ bugs, and they
PLURAL NOUN   ADJECTIVE

were out of their _____ bags in record time! Another time, I hid
                      VERB ENDING IN "ING"

all the rolls of _____ paper in the trunk of Dad's _____,
                 NOUN   NOUN

not knowing that Dad, a/an _____ doctor, was on duty at the
                            ADJECTIVE

_____ that night. But the most _____ prank of all time
NOUN   ADJECTIVE

was when I replaced all of the _____ -paste with _____
                       PART OF THE BODY   ADJECTIVE

icing. When my sister's _____ brushed their _____
                    PLURAL NOUN   PART OF THE BODY (PLURAL)

with it, the _____ looks on their _____ were
           ADJECTIVE   PART OF THE BODY (PLURAL)

priceless—but the _____ icing all over their teeth was even better!
                    COLOR

From SLEEPOVER PARTY MAD LIBS® • Copyright © 2008 by Penguin Random House LLC.

MAD LIBS® is fun to play with friends, but you can also play it by yourself! To begin with, DO NOT look at the story on the page below. Fill in the blanks on this page with the words called for. Then, using the words you have selected, fill in the blank spaces in the story.

Now you've created your own hilarious MAD LIBS® game!

LIGHT AS A FEATHER

_____ ADJECTIVE

_____ ADJECTIVE

_____ ADJECTIVE

_____ ADJECTIVE

_____ NOUN

_____ PLURAL NOUN

_____ PART OF THE BODY (PLURAL)

_____ ADVERB

_____ ADJECTIVE

_____ NUMBER

_____ NOUN

_____ NOUN

_____ NOUN

_____ ADVERB

_____ NOUN

_____ NOUN

_____ ADVERB

_____ PLURAL NOUN

_____ ADJECTIVE

Another _____ sleepover game is _____ as a feather,
          ADJECTIVE   ADJECTIVE

_____ as a board. You'll need a/an _____ volunteer to
 ADJECTIVE   ADJECTIVE

lie down on the _____ with her _____ closed and her
                     NOUN   PLURAL NOUN

_____ folded across her chest. Tell her to breathe
   PART OF THE BODY (PLURAL)

_____ and remain _____ and relaxed. Then gather in a
    ADVERB   ADJECTIVE

circle around her, placing _____ fingers underneath her _____
                              NUMBER   NOUN

as you repeat the phrase, "Light as a/an _____, stiff as a/an
                                              NOUN

_____." On the count of three, _____ lift her off the
   NOUN   ADVERB

_____ and raise her to the _____. Then lower her down
   NOUN   NOUN

_____. Your _____ will be completely amazed at this
    ADVERB   PLURAL NOUN

_____feat!
   ADJECTIVE

MAD LIBS® is fun to play with friends, but you can also play it by yourself! To begin with, DO NOT look at the story on the page below. Fill in the blanks on this page with the words called for. Then, using the words you have selected, fill in the blank spaces in the story.

Now you've created your own hilarious MAD LIBS® game!

LET'S DANCE!

_____ ADJECTIVE

_____ PLURAL NOUN

_____ NUMBER

_____ PLURAL NOUN

_____ ADJECTIVE

_____ ADVERB

_____ ADJECTIVE

_____ NOUN

_____ VERB (PAST TENSE)

_____ PART OF THE BODY

_____ PERSON IN ROOM

_____ ADJECTIVE

_____ NUMBER

_____ PART OF THE BODY

_____ ADVERB

_____ ADJECTIVE

_____ PLURAL NOUN

_____ ADVERB

_____ PLURAL NOUN

_____ NOUN

_____ PART OF THE BODY (PLURAL)

MAD LIBS®

LET'S DANCE!

At my _____ sleepover party, my best _____ and I
         ADJECTIVE   PLURAL NOUN

decided to have a dance-off. We made my _____-year-old little sister be
                                          NUMBER

the judge. We broke into two teams, "The _____" and "The
                                          PLURAL NOUN

_____ Dancers." My team danced _____, but the other
   ADJECTIVE   ADVERB

team's _____ moves were out of this _____! They totally
        ADJECTIVE   NOUN

out-_____ us. So when no one was looking, I grabbed my sister
      VERB (PAST TENSE)

by the _____ and pulled her aside. "_____," I whispered,
       PART OF THE BODY   PERSON IN ROOM

"I promise to do all of your _____ chores for _____ months
                              ADJECTIVE   NUMBER

if you say that my team won." My sister shook her _____. "No
                                                    PART OF THE BODY

way!" she said _____. "Your team danced worse than a bunch of
                ADVERB

_____ _____!" "Fine," I said. "Then I'll just have to tell
   ADJECTIVE   PLURAL NOUN

all of my friends that you're _____ afraid of _____."
                               ADVERB   PLURAL NOUN

That helped to change her _____. We won that contest,
                            NOUN

_____ down!
PART OF THE BODY (PLURAL)

From SLEEPOVER PARTY MAD LIBS® • Copyright © 2008 by Penguin Random House LLC.

SNORE NO MORE

ADJECTIVE _____

NOUN _____

NOUN _____

ADJECTIVE _____

VERB ENDING IN "ING" _____

VERB _____

PART OF THE BODY _____

VERB ENDING IN "ING" _____

ADJECTIVE _____

ADJECTIVE _____

ADJECTIVE _____

VERB ENDING IN "ING" _____

ADJECTIVE _____

ADJECTIVE _____

PART OF THE BODY _____

MAD LIBS®

SNORE NO MORE

Snoring is a loud and often _____ sound that can be compared to
                                    ADJECTIVE

sawing a piece of _____ or to a freight _____ roaring down
                        NOUN   NOUN

the tracks. Fortunately, there are many _____ solutions to keep a
                                              ADJECTIVE

snorer from _____:
              VERB ENDING IN "ING"

1. _____ on your _____ instead of on your back.
      VERB   PART OF THE BODY

2. Try _____ without a/an _____ pillow.
        VERB ENDING IN "ING"   ADJECTIVE

3. Learn to play the didgeridoo, a/an _____ Australian wind
                                            ADJECTIVE

instrument. Studies have shown that this strengthens _____
                                                          ADJECTIVE

airways and helps reduce _____. The trouble with this
                            VERB ENDING IN "ING"

_____ solution is that most people can't stand the
   ADJECTIVE

_____ sound of the didgeridoo.
   ADJECTIVE

4. If all else fails and the snoring continues, buy a pair of _____-
                                                                PART OF THE BODY

plugs for anyone sleeping nearby!

MAD LIBS® is fun to play with friends, but you can also play it by yourself! To begin with, DO NOT look at the story on the page below. Fill in the blanks on this page with the words called for. Then, using the words you have selected, fill in the blank spaces in the story.

Now you've created your own hilarious MAD LIBS® game!

PIZZA PARTY

CELEBRITY _____

ADJECTIVE _____

NUMBER _____

ADJECTIVE _____

PLURAL NOUN _____

PLURAL NOUN _____

NOUN _____

ADJECTIVE _____

PLURAL NOUN _____

PLURAL NOUN _____

ADJECTIVE _____

PLURAL NOUN _____

PLURAL NOUN _____

NOUN _____

MAD LIBS®

PIZZA PARTY

CLERK: Hello, _____'s Pizza Shop. How can I help you?
                    CELEBRITY

GIRL: I'm having a/an _____ party, and I would like to order
                          ADJECTIVE

enough pizza for _____ _____ people.
                     NUMBER   ADJECTIVE

CLERK: Five large _____ should be enough. What
                       PLURAL NOUN

_____ would you like on them? Tonight's special is pizza topped with
   PLURAL NOUN

_____ cheese, _____ tomatoes, and green _____.
       NOUN   ADJECTIVE   PLURAL NOUN

GIRL: Can you add sliced _____ and _____ onions, too?
                              PLURAL NOUN   ADJECTIVE

CLERK: Can do. Since you're ordering more than fifty _____'
                                                          PLURAL NOUN

worth of food, you get free _____ for dessert.
                                PLURAL NOUN

GIRL: Thanks. And please hurry. We're so hungry, we could eat a/an

_____!
      NOUN

MAD LIBS® is fun to play with friends, but you can also play it by yourself! To begin with, DO NOT look at the story on the page below. Fill in the blanks on this page with the words called for. Then, using the words you have selected, fill in the blank spaces in the story.

Now you've created your own hilarious MAD LIBS® game!

NO BOYS ALLOWED!

PERSON IN ROOM (MALE) _____

ADJECTIVE _____

NOUN _____

PLURAL NOUN _____

ADJECTIVE _____

ADJECTIVE _____

ADJECTIVE _____

PART OF THE BODY _____

PLURAL NOUN _____

PART OF THE BODY (PLURAL) _____

PLURAL NOUN _____

MAD LIBS

NO BOYS ALLOWED!

Attention, _____! _____ boys are NOT allowed to
        PERSON IN ROOM (MALE)   ADJECTIVE

enter this room. This ESPECIALLY goes for _____-faced brothers like
                                            NOUN

you! There is a/an _____-only _____ party in progress,
                PLURAL NOUN   ADJECTIVE

and you are not invited. If you dare enter, be aware that you are a target for

_____ pranks. We may even subject you to a/an _____
 ADJECTIVE   ADJECTIVE

makeover and put makeup on your _____ before we let you
                                 PART OF THE BODY

escape. So, if you are made of _____ and snails and puppy-dog
                              PLURAL NOUN

_____, please go back to where you came from. No
  PART OF THE BODY (PLURAL)

_____ allowed!
  PLURAL NOUN

MAD LIBS® is fun to play with friends, but you can also play it by yourself! To begin with, DO NOT look at the story on the page below. Fill in the blanks on this page with the words called for. Then, using the words you have selected, fill in the blank spaces in the story.

Now you've created your own hilarious MAD LIBS® game!

MIDNIGHT MOVIES

_____ ADJECTIVE

_____ ADJECTIVE

_____ PERSON IN ROOM (FEMALE)

_____ NOUN

_____ ADJECTIVE

_____ NOUN

_____ PLURAL NOUN

_____ ADJECTIVE

_____ ADJECTIVE

_____ NOUN

_____ NOUN

_____ PART OF THE BODY

_____ PLURAL NOUN

_____ PERSON IN ROOM (FEMALE)

_____ NOUN

_____ NOUN

_____ ADJECTIVE

_____ NOUN

MAD LIBS

MIDNIGHT MOVIES

Looking for the perfect movie to watch at your sleepover? Try one of these

_____ party favorites:
   ADJECTIVE

• _____ *Girls*: This film stars _____ Lohan as a
   ADJECTIVE   *PERSON IN ROOM (FEMALE)*

homeschooled _____ who goes to a/an _____ high
                        NOUN   *ADJECTIVE*

school for the first time. Will she turn into a mean _____ like the
                                                                        NOUN

rest of the popular _____?
                              PLURAL NOUN

• *Legally* _____: In this movie, a/an _____ sorority
                    ADJECTIVE   *ADJECTIVE*

_____ follows her ex-boyfriend to an Ivy _____ school in
       NOUN   *NOUN*

an attempt to win back his _____.
                                      PART OF THE BODY

• *The Princess* _____: When _____ Thermopolis
                        PLURAL NOUN   *PERSON IN ROOM (FEMALE)*

discovers she is a/an _____ and an heir to the _____ of a/
                              NOUN   *NOUN*

an _____ country, her entire _____ is turned upside down.
       ADJECTIVE   *NOUN*

MAD LIBS® is fun to play with friends, but you can also play it by yourself! To begin with, DO NOT look at the story on the page below. Fill in the blanks on this page with the words called for. Then, using the words you have selected, fill in the blank spaces in the story.

Now you've created your own hilarious MAD LIBS® game!

A GHASTLY GHOST STORY
(PART 1)

_____ ADJECTIVE

_____ PLURAL NOUN

_____ NOUN

_____ NOUN

_____ ADJECTIVE

_____ PLURAL NOUN

_____ NOUN

_____ VERB (PAST TENSE)

_____ ADJECTIVE

_____ NOUN

_____ ADJECTIVE

_____ PART OF THE BODY (PLURAL)

A GHASTLY GHOST STORY
(PART 1)

One dark and _____ night I had a sleepover party with seven
                    ADJECTIVE

_____ at my family's old Victorian _____ at the edge of
   PLURAL NOUN   NOUN

town. I was the first person in the house to fall asleep, and in the middle of the

_____, I was startled awake by a/an _____ sound coming
      NOUN   ADJECTIVE

from the attic. I couldn't stop my _____ from shaking as I slipped into
                                       PLURAL NOUN

a/an _____, _____ upstairs, and opened the door to
           NOUN   VERB (PAST TENSE)

the attic. Out of nowhere, a/an _____ figure in a pale white
                                     ADJECTIVE

_____ with long _____ hair flew past me. Terrified, I
      NOUN   ADJECTIVE

screamed at the top of my _____.
                             PART OF THE BODY (PLURAL)

From SLEEPOVER PARTY MAD LIBS® • Copyright © 2008 by Penguin Random House LLC.

A GHASTLY GHOST STORY (PART 2)

NOUN _____

VERB ENDING IN "ING" _____

NOUN _____

PLURAL NOUN _____

NOUN _____

PART OF THE BODY _____

PLURAL NOUN _____

PLURAL NOUN _____

ADJECTIVE _____

ADJECTIVE _____

ADVERB _____

NOUN _____

NOUN _____

MAD LIBS® is fun to play with friends, but you can also play it by yourself! To begin with, DO NOT look at the story on the page below. Fill in the blanks on this page with the words called for. Then, using the words you have selected, fill in the blank spaces in the story.

Now you've created your own hilarious MAD LIBS® game!

"Relax," said the _____. "You're _____ like a leaf,
                    NOUN   VERB ENDING IN "ING"

but you need not be afraid. I am a friendly _____." "Really?"
                                                     NOUN

I said. "Wow! I can't wait for you to meet my _____."
                                                  PLURAL NOUN

"I would love to, but unfortunately I can only reveal myself to the first

_____ who falls asleep," the ghost replied. And in the blink of a/an
      NOUN

_____, the ghost was gone. I ran to awaken my sleeping
  PART OF THE BODY

_____ to tell them what had happened, but they said they didn't
  PLURAL NOUN

believe me. They told me I'd lost all my _____! But I could tell they
                                              PLURAL NOUN

wished they had seen the _____ ghost. Sure enough, the next time I
                              ADJECTIVE

had a sleepover at my _____ house, each girl tried _____
                           ADJECTIVE   ADVERB

to be the first _____ to fall asleep and meet the friendly
                      NOUN

_____!
     NOUN

MAD LIBS® is fun to play with friends, but you can also play it by yourself! To begin with, DO NOT look at the story on the page below. Fill in the blanks on this page with the words called for. Then, using the words you have selected, fill in the blank spaces in the story.

Now you've created your own hilarious MAD LIBS® game!

HOT FUDGE SUNDAES

_____ NOUN

_____ NUMBER

_____ PLURAL NOUN

_____ ADJECTIVE

_____ ADJECTIVE

_____ ADJECTIVE

_____ NOUN

_____ NUMBER

_____ PLURAL NOUN

_____ NOUN

_____ NOUN

_____ NOUN

_____ VERB (PAST TENSE)

_____ PLURAL NOUN

_____ ADJECTIVE

_____ VERB

MAD LIBS®

HOT FUDGE SUNDAES

Making a hot fudge _____ is as simple as one, two, _____. All you
                         NOUN   NUMBER

need are the following _____:
                         PLURAL NOUN

A pint of _____ ice cream
              ADJECTIVE

1 jar of _____ fudge sauce
              ADJECTIVE

1 cup of _____ nuts
              ADJECTIVE

1 can of whipped _____
                         NOUN

_____ maraschino _____
     NUMBER   PLURAL NOUN

Scoop the ice _____ into a glass _____. Pour on a generous
                    NOUN   NOUN

portion of hot _____ sauce, and add a heaping mound of
                      NOUN

_____ cream. Sprinkle with _____ and top off with
VERB (PAST TENSE)   PLURAL NOUN

a/an _____ cherry. Now _____ and enjoy!
          ADJECTIVE   VERB

MAD LIBS is fun to play with friends, but you can also play it by yourself! To begin with, DO NOT look at the story on the page below. Fill in the blanks on this page with the words called for. Then, using the words you have selected, fill in the blank spaces in the story.

Now you've created your own hilarious MAD LIBS game!

TRUTH OR DARE (PART 1)

NOUN _____

PERSON IN ROOM (MALE) _____

NOUN _____

NUMBER _____

VERB (PAST TENSE) _____

NOUN _____

NUMBER _____

ADJECTIVE _____

VERB _____

NOUN _____

ADJECTIVE _____

NOUN _____

ADJECTIVE _____

TYPE OF LIQUID _____

NOUN _____

PLURAL NOUN _____

TYPE OF LIQUID _____

MAD LIBS

TRUTH OR DARE (PART 1)

Let's play truth or dare! First, some truths:

Q: What is the name of the _____ you like?
NOUN

A: _____.
PERSON IN ROOM (MALE)

Q: What is one _____ no one knows about you?
NOUN

A: When I was _____ years old, I _____ like a/an
NUMBER   VERB (PAST TENSE)

_____ in front of _____ people.
NOUN   NUMBER

Q: If you were stranded on a/an _____ island, what three things
ADJECTIVE

would you bring with you?

A: I couldn't _____ without my precious _____, my
VERB   NOUN

_____ _____, and a/an _____ bottle of
ADJECTIVE   NOUN   ADJECTIVE

_____.
TYPE OF LIQUID

Q: What is the strangest _____ you have ever eaten?
NOUN

A: _____ dipped in _____.
PLURAL NOUN   TYPE OF LIQUID

MAD LIBS® is fun to play with friends, but you can also play it by yourself! To begin with, DO NOT look at the story on the page below. Fill in the blanks on this page with the words called for. Then, using the words you have selected, fill in the blank spaces in the story.

Now you've created your own hilarious MAD LIBS® game!

TRUTH OR DARE (PART 2)

_____ ADJECTIVE

_____ VERB

_____ NOUN

_____ ADJECTIVE

_____ ADJECTIVE

_____ NOUN

_____ NOUN

_____ VERB

_____ PLURAL NOUN

_____ ADJECTIVE

_____ PART OF THE BODY (PLURAL)

_____ NUMBER

MAD LIBS

TRUTH OR DARE (PART 2)

And now for the dares!

DARE: Pretend you are a/an _____ puppy. _____ loudly and
ADJECTIVE   VERB

wag your _____.
NOUN

DARE: Put on some _____ music and dance like a/an
ADJECTIVE

_____ _____ for one minute.
ADJECTIVE   NOUN

DARE: Hop on one _____ while you _____ and say the
NOUN   VERB

alphabet backward.

DARE: Take off your socks and _____ and step into the shower.
PLURAL NOUN

Then turn on the _____ water and yodel at the top of your
ADJECTIVE

_____ for _____ seconds.
PART OF THE BODY (PLURAL)   NUMBER

A BAD NIGHTMARE

PERSON IN ROOM (FEMALE) _____

ADJECTIVE _____

PLURAL NOUN _____

NOUN _____

PLURAL NOUN _____

PLURAL NOUN _____

ADVERB _____

PART OF THE BODY (PLURAL) _____

NOUN _____

NOUN _____

SAME NOUN _____

VERB ENDING IN "ING" _____

VERB ENDING IN "ING" _____

MAD LIBS

A BAD NIGHTMARE

One night when I slept over at my friend _____'s house I had
PERSON IN ROOM (FEMALE)

a/an _____ nightmare that scared the living _____ out of
     ADJECTIVE   PLURAL NOUN

me. I dreamed I was in school, standing in front of my English _____,
                                                                 NOUN

giving a report on Shakespeare's _____, when I realized I wasn't
                                        PLURAL NOUN

wearing any _____. Embarrassed beyond belief, I _____
               PLURAL NOUN   ADVERB

put my hands over my _____ and ran out of the classroom
                          PART OF THE BODY (PLURAL)

at breakneck _____. Suddenly, I was being chased by a wild
                    NOUN

_____! Just as the _____ was about to catch me, I woke up
     NOUN   SAME NOUN

_____ with fright. I spent the rest of the night _____
VERB ENDING IN "ING"   VERB ENDING IN "ING"

with the light on!

MAKEOVER MADNESS

_____
ADJECTIVE

_____
PERSON IN ROOM (FEMALE)

_____
PERSON IN ROOM (FEMALE)

_____
ADJECTIVE

_____
EXCLAMATION

_____
NOUN

_____
PART OF THE BODY

_____
PART OF THE BODY

_____
ADJECTIVE

_____
PLURAL NOUN

_____
NOUN

_____
COLOR

_____
NOUN

_____
PLURAL NOUN

_____
ADJECTIVE

_____
VERB

_____
ADVERB

_____
PLURAL NOUN

_____
NOUN

_____
PART OF THE BODY (PLURAL)

MAD LIBS' is fun to play with friends, but you can also play it by yourself! To begin with, DO NOT look at the story on the page below. Fill in the blanks on this page with the words called for. Then, using the words you have selected, fill in the blank spaces in the story.

Now you've created your own hilarious MAD LIBS' game!

MAD LIBS®

MAKEOVER MADNESS

A/An _____ scene to be played by _____ and
        ADJECTIVE   PERSON IN ROOM (FEMALE)

_____ .
PERSON IN ROOM (FEMALE)

GIRL 1: I'm going to give you a/an _____ makeover.
                                          ADJECTIVE

GIRL 2: _____ ! Will I look like a new _____ ?
            EXCLAMATION   NOUN

GIRL 1: Yes, from head to _____ . First, we'll brush your
                                PART OF THE BODY

_____ to make it sleek and _____ .
   PART OF THE BODY   ADJECTIVE

GIRL 2: What about my _____ ? My friends say my eyes are my best
                             PLURAL NOUN

_____ .
      NOUN

GIRL 1: They are. Applying _____ eye _____ will
                                  COLOR   NOUN

definitely bring out the color of your _____ . And changing your
                                              PLURAL NOUN

_____ clothes will also help.
     ADJECTIVE

GIRL 2: You don't like the way I _____ ?
                                        VERB

GIRL 1: You should try and dress more _____ . Those
                                              ADVERB

_____ you've been wearing are so last year. Trust me, when we're
   PLURAL NOUN

finished, you'll be the talk of the _____ .
                                           NOUN

GIRL 2: I've got my _____ crossed!
                          PART OF THE BODY (PLURAL)

MAD LIBS® is fun to play with friends, but you can also play it by
yourself! To begin with, DO NOT look at the story on the page
below. Fill in the blanks on this page with the words called for. Then,
using the words you have selected, fill in the blank spaces in the story.

Now you've created your own hilarious MAD LIBS® game!

HOW TO SING KARAOKE

ADJECTIVE _____

A PLACE _____

ADVERB _____

NOUN _____

ADJECTIVE _____

ADJECTIVE _____

ADJECTIVE _____

ADJECTIVE _____

ADJECTIVE _____

NOUN _____

ADVERB _____

PLURAL NOUN _____

NOUN _____

MAD LIBS

HOW TO SING KARAOKE

Karaoke is a/an _____ form of entertainment that first became
                         ADJECTIVE

popular in (the) _____ and _____ caught on all over
                     A PLACE   ADVERB

the _____. In karaoke, you sing along to a/an _____ song
        NOUN   ADJECTIVE

using a/an _____ microphone. You don't have to be a particularly
              ADJECTIVE

good singer to sing karaoke—you can even be a/an _____ singer.
                                                        ADJECTIVE

The most important thing is to have a/an _____ time. Karaoke is
                                              ADJECTIVE

especially _____ at a sleepover party. You don't even need a/an
               ADJECTIVE

_____ machine! You can just turn up the radio and sing
      NOUN

_____. Just be sure to give other _____ a turn—you don't
      ADVERB   PLURAL NOUN

want to be a/an _____ hog!
                     NOUN

SLEEPOVER, SCHMEEPOVER

ADJECTIVE _____

PLURAL NOUN _____

NUMBER _____

NOUN _____

NUMBER _____

NOUN _____

NOUN _____

PLURAL NOUN _____

NOUN _____

PLURAL NOUN _____

PLURAL NOUN _____

NOUN _____

PLURAL NOUN _____

ADJECTIVE _____

NOUN _____

MAD LIBS® is fun to play with friends, but you can also play it by yourself! To begin with, DO NOT look at the story on the page below. Fill in the blanks on this page with the words called for. Then, using the words you have selected, fill in the blank spaces in the story.

Now you've created your own hilarious MAD LIBS® game!

MAD LIBS

SLEEPOVER, SCHMEEPOVER

The _____ thing about sleepover parties is that, even though you're
          ADJECTIVE

supposed to "sleep over," chances are you and your _____ will catch
                                                    PLURAL NOUN

fewer than _____ winks! It's always the same—you promise your mom
            NUMBER

and _____ that you'll go to bed before _____ o'clock, but
      NOUN   NUMBER

instead you stay up until the crack of _____. The next thing you
                                         NOUN

know, you're waking up to the smell of fried _____ and scrambled
                                               NOUN

_____ emanating from the _____. After breakfast, you
   PLURAL NOUN   NOUN

change out of your _____, pack your _____, and stumble into
                     PLURAL NOUN   PLURAL NOUN

your parents' _____ when they come to pick you up. If you're like
                 NOUN

most _____ your age, you'll be so tired, you'll want to take a/an
       PLURAL NOUN

_____ nap the minute you get home. Which gets a/an
   ADJECTIVE

_____ thinking—maybe they should call them awake-overs instead!
   NOUN

From SLEEPOVER PARTY MAD LIBS® • Copyright © 2008 by Penguin Random House LLC.

MAD LIBS®

GRAND SLAM
MAD LIBS

by Roger Price and Leonard Stern

MAD LIBS®

INSTRUCTIONS

MAD LIBS® is a game for people who don't like games!
It can be played by one, two, three, four, or forty.

● RIDICULOUSLY SIMPLE DIRECTIONS

In this tablet you will find stories containing blank spaces where words are left out. One player, the READER, selects one of these stories. The READER does not tell anyone what the story is about. Instead, he/she asks the other players, the WRITERS, to give him/her words. These words are used to fill in the blank spaces in the story.

● TO PLAY

The READER asks each WRITER in turn to call out a word—an adjective or a noun or whatever the space calls for—and uses them to fill in the blank spaces in the story. The result is a MAD LIBS® game.

When the READER then reads the completed MAD LIBS® game to the other players, they will discover that they have written a story that is fantastic, screamingly funny, shocking, silly, crazy, or just plain dumb—depending upon which words each WRITER called out.

● EXAMPLE (Before and After)

"_____!" he said _____
     EXCLAMATION   ADVERB

as he jumped into his convertible _____ and
                                   NOUN

drove off with his _____ wife.
                    ADJECTIVE

"*Ouch*!" he said *stupidly*
     EXCLAMATION   ADVERB

as he jumped into his convertible *cat* and
                               NOUN

drove off with his *brave* wife.
                   ADJECTIVE

MAD LIBS®

QUICK REVIEW

In case you have forgotten what adjectives, adverbs, nouns, and verbs are, here is a quick review:

An ADJECTIVE describes something or somebody. *Lumpy, soft, ugly, messy,* and *short* are adjectives.

An ADVERB tells how something is done. It modifies a verb and usually ends in "ly." *Modestly, stupidly, greedily,* and *carefully* are adverbs.

A NOUN is the name of a person, place, or thing. *Sidewalk, umbrella, bridle, bathtub,* and *nose* are nouns.

A VERB is an action word. *Run, pitch, jump,* and *swim* are verbs. Put the verbs in past tense if the directions say PAST TENSE. *Ran, pitched, jumped,* and *swam* are verbs in the past tense.

When we ask for A PLACE, we mean any sort of place: a country or city *(Spain, Cleveland)* or a room *(bathroom, kitchen).*

An EXCLAMATION or SILLY WORD is any sort of funny sound, gasp, grunt, or outcry, like *Wow!, Ouch!, Whomp!, Ick!,* and *Gadzooks!*

When we ask for specific words, like a NUMBER, a COLOR, an ANIMAL, or a PART OF THE BODY, we mean a word that is one of those things, like *seven, blue, horse,* or *head.*

When we ask for a PLURAL, it means more than one. For example, *cat* pluralized is *cats.*

MAD LIBS® is fun to play with friends, but you can also play it by yourself! To begin with, DO NOT look at the story on the page below. Fill in the blanks on this page with the words called for. Then, using the words you have selected, fill in the blank spaces in the story.

Now you've created your own hilarious MAD LIBS® game!

THE FRIENDLY GAME OF BASEBALL

ADJECTIVE _____

ADJECTIVE _____

ADJECTIVE _____

NOUN _____

NUMBER _____

NUMBER _____

NOUN _____

A PLACE _____

NOUN _____

NOUN _____

ADVERB _____

OCCUPATION _____

VERB _____

PLURAL NOUN _____

PLURAL NOUN _____

NOUN _____

ADJECTIVE _____

A PLACE _____

MAD LIBS®

THE FRIENDLY GAME OF BASEBALL

Are you a/an _____ athlete looking for something
                    ADJECTIVE

_____ to do after school? Why not learn how to play the
   ADJECTIVE

_____ game of baseball? Baseball is played on a field shaped like
   ADJECTIVE

a/an _____. There are _____ teams in a league, and
        NOUN   NUMBER

each team is limited to _____ players. The teams take turns going
                          NUMBER

to bat at the _____ and playing defense in (the) _____.
                NOUN   A PLACE

The batting team sends players up to home-_____ one at a time.
                                            NOUN

Each player tries to hit the _____ as _____ as he can
                              NOUN   ADVERB

and then run to first base without being tagged out by the _____.
                                                            OCCUPATION

If the player can _____ around all the bases, he scores! When you
                   VERB

score in baseball, you score _____, and the team with the most
                              PLURAL NOUN

_____ wins the _____. Baseball is simple, it's exciting,
   PLURAL NOUN   NOUN

and it's _____. No wonder it's (the) _____'s favorite
          ADJECTIVE   A PLACE

pastime!

MAD LIBS® is fun to play with friends, but you can also play it by yourself! To begin with, DO NOT look at the story on the page below. Fill in the blanks on this page with the words called for. Then, using the words you have selected, fill in the blank spaces in the story.

Now you've created your own hilarious MAD LIBS® game!

SPRING TRAINING

A PLACE _____

ADJECTIVE _____

ADJECTIVE _____

ADJECTIVE _____

A PLACE _____

PLURAL NOUN _____

A PLACE _____

PLURAL NOUN _____

NOUN _____

PLURAL NOUN _____

A PLACE _____

PLURAL NOUN _____

ADJECTIVE _____

PERSON IN ROOM _____

NUMBER _____

PLURAL NOUN _____

ADJECTIVE _____

NOUN _____

PLURAL NOUN _____

ADVERB _____

NOUN _____

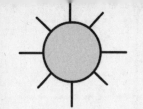

MAD LIBS

SPRING TRAINING

My trip to (the) _____ for baseball spring training was
                    A PLACE

_____! I went with my buddy, who is a/an
         ADJECTIVE

_____ fan—just like me. On the first day, we
       ADJECTIVE

watched a/an _____ exhibition game between (the)
                   ADJECTIVE

_____ _____ and (the) _____
    A PLACE   PLURAL NOUN   A PLACE

_____. Throughout the entire _____
   PLURAL NOUN   NOUN

we were on the edge of our _____! The next day, we
                               PLURAL NOUN

watched (the) _____ _____ hold batting and
                  A PLACE   PLURAL NOUN

fielding practice. We quickly learned what a/an _____
                                                     ADJECTIVE

athlete _____ is. He hit _____ home
           PERSON IN ROOM   NUMBER

_____! Not only is he a power hitter, he is also a/an
   PLURAL NOUN

_____ defensive first _____. After practice, I asked
   ADJECTIVE   NOUN

him to autograph one of the _____ I had with me, which he
                                PLURAL NOUN

did _____. It's now on display in my room, right next to my
       ADVERB

_____ collection!
   NOUN

RECORD BREAKERS

PLURAL NOUN _____

ADJECTIVE _____

NOUN _____

ADJECTIVE _____

ADJECTIVE _____

PERSON IN ROOM _____

ADJECTIVE _____

PLURAL NOUN _____

PERSON IN ROOM _____

ADJECTIVE _____

VERB ENDING IN "ING" _____

PERSON IN ROOM _____

NOUN _____

ADJECTIVE _____

NOUN _____

OCCUPATION _____

ADVERB _____

NOUN _____

ADJECTIVE _____

PART OF THE BODY _____

MAD LIBS® is fun to play with friends, but you can also play it by yourself! To begin with, DO NOT look at the story on the page below. Fill in the blanks on this page with the words called for. Then, using the words you have selected, fill in the blank spaces in the story.

Now you've created your own hilarious MAD LIBS® game!

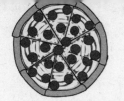

MAD LIBS

RECORD BREAKERS

To celebrate our little league team's many _____ this season, our
                                              PLURAL NOUN

coach took us to a/an _____ restaurant for a pizza party. At the
                           ADJECTIVE

_____, he gave out _____ awards to our team's most
      NOUN   ADJECTIVE

_____ players. _____ got the "_____
      ADJECTIVE   PERSON IN ROOM   ADJECTIVE

Slugger" award for hitting the most home _____.
                                              PLURAL NOUN

_____ won the "_____ Eye" award for having the
  PERSON IN ROOM   ADJECTIVE

best _____ average. _____ set a new record for
     VERB ENDING IN "ING"   PERSON IN ROOM

_____ stealing, and was given a/an _____ trophy.
      NOUN   ADJECTIVE

I wasn't sure if Coach had a/an _____ for me. I knew I wasn't
                                      NOUN

the best hitter or the best _____—though I worked very
                                OCCUPATION

_____ all season. But, to my surprise, Coach gave me a small silver
   ADVERB

_____ for being a/an _____ team player. I'm so proud,
      NOUN   ADJECTIVE

I can't wipe the smile off my _____!
                                 PART OF THE BODY

RIGHT THROUGH HIS LEGS

_____ NOUN

_____ COLOR

_____ PLURAL NOUN

_____ A PLACE

_____ PLURAL NOUN

_____ CELEBRITY

_____ NOUN

_____ NOUN

_____ CELEBRITY

_____ ADJECTIVE

_____ NOUN

_____ ADJECTIVE

_____ PLURAL NOUN

_____ EXCLAMATION

_____ NOUN

_____ ADJECTIVE

_____ ADJECTIVE

_____ PLURAL NOUN

MAD LIBS®

RIGHT THROUGH HIS LEGS

It was game six of the _____ Series, 1986. The Boston
                              NOUN

_____ _____ were tied with (the)
    COLOR   PLURAL NOUN

_____ _____ in the bottom of the
   A PLACE   PLURAL NOUN

tenth inning when _____ stepped up to the plate. There
                CELEBRITY

were two outs and a/an _____ on third. All Boston needed
                NOUN

was one more _____ to bring home a victory.
             NOUN

_____, a/an _____ sinker-ball pitcher,
   CELEBRITY   ADJECTIVE

threw a terrific _____. Getting the batter out should
             NOUN

have been as _____ as 1-2-3, but the ball went right
         ADJECTIVE

through the first baseman's _____. Cries of "Oh no!" and
                PLURAL NOUN

"_____!" were heard throughout the stands. The player on
   EXCLAMATION

third raced home and scored the winning _____. To this
                        NOUN

day, _____ baseball fans still talk about that game and the
     ADJECTIVE

_____ loss for the Red _____.
  ADJECTIVE   PLURAL NOUN

MAD LIBS® is fun to play with friends, but you can also play it by yourself! To begin with, DO NOT look at the story on the page below. Fill in the blanks on this page with the words called for. Then, using the words you have selected, fill in the blank spaces in the story.

Now you've created your own hilarious MAD LIBS® game!

PLAYIN' BY THE RULES

_____ NOUN

_____ PLURAL NOUN

_____ ADJECTIVE

_____ NOUN

_____ NOUN

_____ NOUN

_____ PLURAL NOUN

_____ PART OF THE BODY

_____ NOUN

_____ VERB (PAST TENSE)

_____ NOUN

_____ NOUN

_____ VERB ENDING IN "S"

_____ A PLACE

_____ ADJECTIVE

_____ PLURAL NOUN

_____ ADJECTIVE

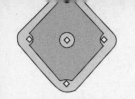

MAD LIBS®

PLAYIN' BY THE RULES

We all know the basic rules of baseball—each team tries to hit the

_____ and score as many _____ as
NOUN   PLURAL NOUN

possible. However, there are many _____ rules that
                                   ADJECTIVE

even a knowledgeable _____ might not know. For
                      NOUN

example, there's the Infield _____ Rule, which states
                              NOUN

that when a player hits a pop _____ into the infield,
                               NOUN

and there are _____ on base, the player is automatically out.
              PLURAL NOUN

The umpire throws his _____ into the air and shouts, "Infield
                       PART OF THE BODY

fly, _____ out!" Another lesser-known rule of baseball is the
      NOUN

_____ Third Strike Rule. This rule is used when the catcher
VERB (PAST TENSE)

fails to catch a/an _____ for a third strike. The umpire shouts,
                     NOUN

"_____ still in play!" The batter _____ as fast
  NOUN   VERB ENDING IN "S"

as he can, all the way to (the) _____. Now that you know these
                                 A PLACE

_____ rules, you can go out to the ballpark and impress all your
ADJECTIVE

_____ with your _____ knowledge!
PLURAL NOUN   ADJECTIVE

From GRAND SLAM MAD LIBS® • Copyright © 2009 by Penguin Random House LLC.

MAD LIBS® is fun to play with friends, but you can also play it by yourself! To begin with, DO NOT look at the story on the page below. Fill in the blanks on this page with the words called for. Then, using the words you have selected, fill in the blank spaces in the story.

Now you've created your own hilarious MAD LIBS® game!

GIMME A SIGN

ADJECTIVE _____

PLURAL NOUN _____

NUMBER _____

PART OF THE BODY _____

NOUN _____

PART OF THE BODY (PLURAL) _____

ADJECTIVE _____

NOUN _____

EXCLAMATION _____

VERB (PAST TENSE) _____

PLURAL NOUN _____

PLURAL NOUN _____

NOUN _____

PART OF THE BODY _____

VERB _____

ADVERB _____

NOUN _____

NOUN _____

MAD LIBS

GIMME A SIGN

Being a catcher isn't as _____ as it looks. Not only do I have to catch
_____ADJECTIVE_____

_____ coming at me at _____ miles an hour—I also have to
___PLURAL NOUN___ ___NUMBER___

use _____ signals to tell the pitcher which _____ to throw,
___PART OF THE BODY___ ___NOUN___

and those are hard to memorize! Yesterday, for example, I wanted the first pitch

to be a fastball, so I pointed two _____ to the ground. To
___PART OF THE BODY (PLURAL)___

my surprise, the _____ pitcher threw a/an _____-ball!
___ADJECTIVE___ ___NOUN___

"_____!" I cried as the ball _____ right past me,
___EXCLAMATION___ ___VERB (PAST TENSE)___

allowing all the _____ to advance. Then, when there were two
___PLURAL NOUN___

_____ on base and their cleanup _____ was at bat,
___PLURAL NOUN___ ___NOUN___

I pointed my _____ to the ground, which means "Intentional
___PART OF THE BODY___

_____." But instead of _____ walking the batter,
___VERB___ ___ADVERB___

the pitcher threw a curveball. The batter hit it over the fence, and we lost the

_____. As you can see, a catcher's _____ is not an
___NOUN___ ___NOUN___

easy one!

MAD LIBS® is fun to play with friends, but you can also play it by yourself! To begin with, DO NOT look at the story on the page below. Fill in the blanks on this page with the words called for. Then, using the words you have selected, fill in the blank spaces in the story.

Now you've created your own hilarious MAD LIBS® game!

BASEBALL'S BIGGEST FAN

_____ PLURAL NOUN

_____ PLURAL NOUN

_____ NOUN

_____ NOUN

_____ NOUN

_____ CELEBRITY

_____ ADJECTIVE

_____ PLURAL NOUN

_____ NOUN

_____ ADJECTIVE

_____ NOUN

_____ NOUN

_____ ADJECTIVE

_____ ADJECTIVE

_____ NOUN

_____ ADVERB

_____ NOUN

MAD LIBS

BASEBALL'S BIGGEST FAN

I am the world's biggest fan of the game of baseball—whether it's played

by professional _____ or little league _____.
                        PLURAL NOUN   PLURAL NOUN

I watch all the games on a big-screen _____ in our
                                                NOUN

family _____. I have a/an _____ autographed
            NOUN   NOUN

by _____, the most _____ player who ever
        CELEBRITY   ADJECTIVE

lived. I even named my dog _____ after my favorite
                                PLURAL NOUN

_____. And when my _____ parents asked
        NOUN   ADJECTIVE

me where I'd like to go this year on vacation, I said, "Cooperstown,

of course, so I can visit the Baseball Hall of _____." This year for
                                                    NOUN

my birthday I'm hoping to get a thirty-two-inch baseball _____
                                                                NOUN

made of northern white ash—just like the _____ sluggers use.
                                                ADJECTIVE

Some people go through life seeking _____ wisdom and asking
                                            ADJECTIVE

questions like "What's the meaning of _____?" and "What's the
                                            NOUN

secret to living _____?" All I want to know is, "Who's pitching and
                    ADVERB

who's on _____?"
            NOUN

SPORTY SUPERSTITIONS

NOUN
_____

PLURAL NOUN
_____

PERSON IN ROOM
_____

NOUN
_____

ADJECTIVE
_____

ADJECTIVE
_____

ADJECTIVE
_____

PLURAL NOUN
_____

PERSON IN ROOM
_____

VERB
_____

NUMBER
_____

NOUN
_____

VERB ENDING IN "ING"
_____

PERSON IN ROOM
_____

PART OF THE BODY
_____

ARTICLE OF CLOTHING
_____

NUMBER
_____

PLURAL NOUN
_____

NOUN
_____

Now you've created your own hilarious MAD LIBS® game!

MAD LIBS® is fun to play with friends, but you can also play it by yourself! To begin with, DO NOT look at the story on the page below. Fill in the blanks on this page with the words called for. Then, using the words you have selected, fill in the blank spaces in the story.

MAD LIBS®

SPORTY SUPERSTITIONS

Our little league _____ is on a winning streak, and some of the
                         NOUN

_____ on the team are getting superstitious. _____ always
   PLURAL NOUN   PERSON IN ROOM

puts a four- _____ inside his/her baseball cap for _____.
                  NOUN   ADJECTIVE

It sounds _____, but he/she keeps catching _____
               ADJECTIVE   ADJECTIVE

high fly _____! _____ convinced that he/she needs to
            PLURAL NOUN   PERSON IN ROOM

_____ in a circle _____ times before stepping up to the
      VERB   NUMBER

_____. It works. He/She has the best _____ average on
      NOUN   VERB ENDING IN "ING"

the team. _____'s superstitions have gotten out of _____.
             PERSON IN ROOM   PART OF THE BODY

He/She has worn the same dirty _____ for _____ games
                                  ARTICLE OF CLOTHING   NUMBER

in a row! I like to win, but if it means sitting in a dugout that smells like rotten

_____, that's going beyond the call _____!
   PLURAL NOUN   NOUN

MAD LIBS® is fun to play with friends, but you can also play it by yourself! To begin with, DO NOT look at the story on the page below. Fill in the blanks on this page with the words called for. Then, using the words you have selected, fill in the blank spaces in the story.

Now you've created your own hilarious MAD LIBS® game!

TAKE ME OUT

ADJECTIVE _____

ADJECTIVE _____

VERB _____

NOUN _____

NOUN _____

TYPE OF FOOD (PLURAL) _____

PLURAL NOUN _____

ADJECTIVE _____

VERB _____

ADJECTIVE _____

VERB _____

NUMBER _____

ADJECTIVE _____

MAD LIBS®

TAKE ME OUT

Every _____ baseball game follows the _____ tradition
         ADJECTIVE   ADJECTIVE

of the seventh-inning stretch. Midway through the seventh inning, you stand

up, _____, and sing this famous song:
         VERB

"Take me out to the ball _____.
                              NOUN

Take me out with the _____.
                          NOUN

Buy me some _____ and _____.
               TYPE OF FOOD (PLURAL)   PLURAL NOUN

I don't care if I ever get _____.
                               ADJECTIVE

For it's root, root, _____ for the _____ team.
                          VERB   ADJECTIVE

If they don't _____ it's a shame.
                   VERB

For it's one! Two! _____ strikes, you're out at the
                          NUMBER

_____ ball game!"
   ADJECTIVE

LITTLE LEAGUE HERO

ADVERB _____

PERSON IN ROOM _____

VERB _____

A PLACE _____

PLURAL NOUN _____

ADVERB _____

PLURAL NOUN _____

NOUN _____

PART OF THE BODY (PLURAL) _____

NOUN _____

NOUN _____

NOUN _____

NOUN _____

ADJECTIVE _____

PART OF THE BODY _____

VERB _____

PERSON IN ROOM _____

PART OF THE BODY (PLURAL) _____

ADJECTIVE _____

Now you've created your own hilarious MAD LIBS® game!

MAD LIBS® is fun to play with friends, but you can also play it by yourself! To begin with, DO NOT look at the story on the page below. Fill in the blanks on this page with the words called for. Then, using the words you have selected, fill in the blank spaces in the story.

MAD LIBS®

LITTLE LEAGUE HERO

Even though I practiced _____ all season long and never missed
                          ADVERB

any practices, Coach _____ didn't think I was ready to
                     PERSON IN ROOM

_____ in a real game. I finally got my shot. (The)
      VERB

_____ _____ were beating us
   A PLACE   PLURAL NOUN

_____, and our best player was injured. So in the
    ADVERB

ninth inning, with two outs and the _____ loaded, the coach's
                                      PLURAL NOUN

eyes searched the bench for a pinch _____. His
                                           NOUN

_____ fell on me. He gave me the nod. I reached for
PART OF THE BODY (PLURAL)

my _____, raced to the plate, and gave the pitcher my most
      NOUN

_____ stare. The pitcher threw a fast-_____.
   ADJECTIVE   NOUN

I swung and hit it out of the _____ for a grand-slam home
                                    NOUN

_____. The crowd went _____! As I ran the bases, my
      NOUN   ADJECTIVE

teammates patted me on the _____ and shouted, "Way to
                              PART OF THE BODY

_____, _____!" Then they carried me off the
      VERB   PERSON IN ROOM

field on their _____. It was the most _____
               PART OF THE BODY (PLURAL)   ADJECTIVE

moment of my life!

MAD LIBS® is fun to play with friends, but you can also play it by yourself! To begin with, DO NOT look at the story on the page below. Fill in the blanks on this page with the words called for. Then, using the words you have selected, fill in the blank spaces in the story.

Now you've created your own hilarious MAD LIBS® game!

THE CURSE OF
THE BILLY GOAT

ANIMAL (PLURAL) _____

VERB ENDING IN "ING" _____

ADJECTIVE _____

PERSON IN ROOM _____

PLURAL NOUN _____

ADJECTIVE _____

ADJECTIVE _____

PLURAL NOUN _____

NOUN _____

ADJECTIVE _____

ADJECTIVE _____

ADVERB _____

NOUN _____

ADJECTIVE _____

ADJECTIVE _____

ADVERB _____

NOUN _____

MAD LIBS®

THE CURSE OF THE BILLY GOAT

The Chicago _____ are famous for their bad luck
ANIMAL (PLURAL)

and long _____ streaks. Many people call it a/an
VERB ENDING IN "ING"

_____ curse. As the story goes, _____,
ADJECTIVE   PERSON IN ROOM

an immigrant from Transylvania, had two tickets to the 1945

World Series against the Detroit _____. Having no
PLURAL NOUN

place to leave his _____ pet goat, Dracula, he brought
ADJECTIVE

it to the ballpark. Unfortunately, before the _____
ADJECTIVE

game was over, it started to rain cats and _____.
PLURAL NOUN

The goat, soaked to the _____, began to smell so
NOUN

_____ that the owner of the _____ baseball
ADJECTIVE   ADJECTIVE

team _____ ordered the goat out of the stadium.
ADVERB

The owner of the goat was madder than a/an _____
NOUN

and said he was putting a/an _____ curse on the
ADJECTIVE

_____ team. To this day, that team still struggles
ADJECTIVE

_____ in postseason play. They haven't won
ADVERB

a/an _____ Series since 1908!
NOUN

MAD LIBS® is fun to play with friends, but you can also play it by yourself! To begin with, DO NOT look at the story on the page below. Fill in the blanks on this page with the words called for. Then, using the words you have selected, fill in the blank spaces in the story.

Now you've created your own hilarious MAD LIBS® game!

BASEBALL CARDS

PLURAL NOUN _____

ADJECTIVE _____

NOUN _____

PLURAL NOUN _____

PERSON IN ROOM _____

CELEBRITY _____

CELEBRITY _____

EXCLAMATION _____

ADJECTIVE _____

PLURAL NOUN _____

ADJECTIVE _____

ADVERB _____

NUMBER _____

PLURAL NOUN _____

ADJECTIVE _____

VERB ENDING IN "ING" _____

CELEBRITY _____

NOUN _____

PLURAL NOUN _____

MAD LIBS®

BASEBALL CARDS

I've been collecting baseball _____ for years. I started my
                                PLURAL NOUN

collection by buying a/an _____ pack of cards at the local
                          ADJECTIVE

_____ store. I kept the cards I liked and traded the ones
     NOUN

I didn't for new _____. I made my first trade at my friend
                  PLURAL NOUN

_____'s house. I gave him my 2005 _____ in
 PERSON IN ROOM   CELEBRITY

exchange for his 1999 _____. "_____!"
                       CELEBRITY   EXCLAMATION

I thought, "What a/an _____ trade!" Every weekend I would
                      ADJECTIVE

go to swap _____ and trade with _____
           PLURAL NOUN   ADJECTIVE

collectors. My collection grew _____. I now have
                               ADVERB

over _____ cards! I put the valuable ones in plastic
     NUMBER

_____ to keep them in _____ condition and
 PLURAL NOUN   ADJECTIVE

preserve their _____ value. My favorite card, however, is
               VERB ENDING IN "ING"

my 2002 _____. My dad says to guard it with my
        CELEBRITY

_____—it's going to be worth hundreds of _____
 NOUN   PLURAL NOUN

someday!

RIVALRY

_____ PLURAL NOUN

_____ NOUN

_____ NUMBER

_____ ADVERB

_____ ADJECTIVE

_____ PERSON IN ROOM (MALE)

_____ ADJECTIVE

_____ PLURAL NOUN

_____ ADJECTIVE

_____ PERSON IN ROOM

_____ ADJECTIVE

_____ ADJECTIVE

_____ NOUN

_____ VERB ENDING IN "ING"

_____ ADJECTIVE

_____ PLURAL NOUN

MAD LIBS

RIVALRY

The _____, our biggest rivals, think they're better
      PLURAL NOUN

than everyone else just because they've won the _____
                                                         NOUN

championship _____ times. They also _____ beat us in
                NUMBER   ADVERB

every _____ game last season. The only reason they won
         ADJECTIVE

is because they had _____ on their team, the
                       PERSON IN ROOM (MALE)

best _____ pitcher in the league. But he isn't playing
        ADJECTIVE

this year, so we've got a chance to beat the _____ off
                                                PLURAL NOUN

'em. And this year we've got some really _____ players.
                                             ADJECTIVE

_____, our _____ fielder, can throw all the
PERSON IN ROOM   ADJECTIVE

way from _____ field to first _____! Also,
            ADJECTIVE   NOUN

I've been going to the batting cages every Saturday to practice my

_____ skills, so I won't strike out so much anymore. I can't wait
VERB ENDING IN "ING"

for the _____ game against our rivals this Saturday. We'll give 'em a
           ADJECTIVE

run for their _____!
                 PLURAL NOUN

MAD LIBS® is fun to play with friends, but you can also play it by yourself! To begin with, DO NOT look at the story on the page below. Fill in the blanks on this page with the words called for. Then, using the words you have selected, fill in the blank spaces in the story.

Now you've created your own hilarious MAD LIBS® game!

COACH'S PEP TALK

PLURAL NOUN _____

NUMBER _____

ADJECTIVE _____

NOUN _____

ADJECTIVE _____

NOUN _____

EXCLAMATION _____

PART OF THE BODY _____

ADJECTIVE _____

NOUN _____

ADVERB _____

PART OF THE BODY (PLURAL) _____

NOUN _____

NOUN _____

MAD LIBS®

COACH'S PEP TALK

All right, _____! Listen up! It's the bottom of the ninth, and
        PLURAL NOUN

we're down by _____ runs. Okay, we know our opponents are a
        NUMBER

very _____ team and they're on a winning _____
    ADJECTIVE   NOUN

right now, but we can beat them. Some might say it would take a/an

_____ miracle for us to score a single _____. To that
   ADJECTIVE   NOUN

I say: _____! We all put our pants on one _____
     EXCLAMATION   PART OF THE BODY

at a time. It ain't over till the _____ lady sings! We can still win this
                       ADJECTIVE

_____ provided you think _____ and play your
   NOUN   ADVERB

_____ out! Remember, you can do anything you put
 PART OF THE BODY (PLURAL)

your _____ to. Now let's get out there and give it our best
       NOUN

_____!
   NOUN

BALLPARK CUISINE

ADJECTIVE _____

TYPE OF LIQUID _____

NOUN _____

PLURAL NOUN _____

PLURAL NOUN _____

PLURAL NOUN _____

PLURAL NOUN _____

NOUN _____

ADJECTIVE _____

VERB _____

NOUN _____

PLURAL NOUN _____

ADJECTIVE _____

ADJECTIVE _____

ADJECTIVE _____

PLURAL NOUN _____

ADJECTIVE _____

ADJECTIVE _____

MAD LIBS® is fun to play with friends, but you can also play it by yourself! To begin with, DO NOT look at the story on the page below. Fill in the blanks on this page with the words called for. Then, using the words you have selected, fill in the blank spaces in the story.

Now you've created your own hilarious MAD LIBS® game!

MAD LIBS®

BALLPARK CUISINE

Ah, there's nothing better than sitting in the _____
ADJECTIVE

bleachers with a cold cup of _____ and a hot ballpark
TYPE OF LIQUID

_____ topped with mustard, sauerkraut, and lots of
NOUN

_____. Today, the food _____ at many
PLURAL NOUN   PLURAL NOUN

ballparks are like five-star _____, serving everything
PLURAL NOUN

from soup to _____. But to the true baseball
PLURAL NOUN

_____, the best stuff is sold by the _____
NOUN   ADJECTIVE

vendors, who _____ around the aisles shouting, "Get your ice-
VERB

cold _____! Get your roasted _____!" But
NOUN   PLURAL NOUN

_____ dogs and cold _____ soda remain the favorite
ADJECTIVE   ADJECTIVE

_____ food of baseball _____. Some might argue
ADJECTIVE   PLURAL NOUN

the best part of going to a/an _____ game is the delicious,
ADJECTIVE

_____ cuisine!
ADJECTIVE

MAD LIBS® is fun to play with friends, but you can also play it by yourself! To begin with, DO NOT look at the story on the page below. Fill in the blanks on this page with the words called for. Then, using the words you have selected, fill in the blank spaces in the story.

Now you've created your own hilarious MAD LIBS® game!

SLIDERS, SINKERS, AND CURVEBALLS

ADJECTIVE _____

PLURAL NOUN _____

NOUN _____

PART OF THE BODY _____

NOUN _____

NOUN _____

NOUN _____

NOUN _____

NOUN _____

NOUN _____

NOUN _____

PLURAL NOUN _____

PLURAL NOUN _____

PART OF THE BODY _____

NOUN _____

NOUN _____

NOUN _____

MAD LIBS®

SLIDERS, SINKERS, AND CURVEBALLS

A/An _____ pitcher today can throw a variety of
    ADJECTIVE

_____, each of which has a slightly different velocity
   PLURAL NOUN

and _____, determined by the way he holds the ball in his
        NOUN

_____. The fast-_____ is the most common
   PART OF THE BODY   NOUN

_____ in baseball and can come toward a batter faster than a speeding
   NOUN

_____, often registering ninety-five miles per _____ on the
   NOUN   NOUN

radar _____. If a pitcher alternates a fast-_____ with an
         NOUN   NOUN

off-speed pitch one called a curve or a breaking _____, he can
                                                        NOUN

tie a batter up in _____. And, if his bag of _____
                      PLURAL NOUN   PLURAL NOUN

includes a split _____ fastball and a knuckle-
                      PART OF THE BODY

_____, he is bound to be a twenty _____
       NOUN   NOUN

winner and will probably end up in the Baseball Hall of _____!
                                                             NOUN

MAD LIBS® is fun to play with friends, but you can also play it by yourself! To begin with, DO NOT look at the story on the page below. Fill in the blanks on this page with the words called for. Then, using the words you have selected, fill in the blank spaces in the story.

Now you've created your own hilarious MAD LIBS® game!

THREE CHEERS
FOR THE UNDERDOG

_____ CELEBRITY

_____ A PLACE

_____ ADJECTIVE

_____ PART OF THE BODY

_____ VERB

_____ PERSON IN ROOM

_____ ADJECTIVE

_____ VERB

_____ NOUN

_____ ADJECTIVE

_____ PLURAL NOUN

_____ ADJECTIVE

_____ ADJECTIVE

_____ PERSON IN ROOM

_____ A PLACE

_____ PLURAL NOUN

_____ PLURAL NOUN

_____ PART OF THE BODY

MAD LIBS

THREE CHEERS FOR THE UNDERDOG

Few people gave _____ High School any chance of advancing
CELEBRITY

to (the) _____ championships because of all the obstacles they
A PLACE

faced throughout the _____ season. Their best hitter broke his
ADJECTIVE

_____ during the first week. Their star catcher quit the team
PART OF THE BODY

in order to _____ in the school's stage production of *Romeo*
VERB

and _____. On top of that, a/an _____ flood
PERSON IN ROOM   ADJECTIVE

ruined the school's practice field, forcing the team to _____ inside the
VERB

_____ for three weeks! But with _____ work and determination,
NOUN   ADJECTIVE

these young _____ found a way to win the _____ regional
PLURAL NOUN   ADJECTIVE

playoffs, and bring home a/an _____ trophy. How does Coach
ADJECTIVE

_____ think they'll do in the state championship game against (the)
PERSON IN ROOM

_____ _____ next week? "Oh we'll give them a run for
A PLACE   PLURAL NOUN

their _____, that's for sure. This team has a lot of _____!"
PLURAL NOUN   PART OF THE BODY

CURSE OF THE BAMBINO

COLOR _____

PLURAL NOUN _____

LAST NAME _____

PLURAL NOUN _____

ADVERB _____

PLURAL NOUN _____

ADVERB _____

NOUN _____

PART OF THE BODY _____

ADVERB _____

VERB ENDING IN "ING" _____

NOUN _____

PLURAL NOUN _____

PLURAL NOUN _____

PERSON IN ROOM _____

ADJECTIVE _____

This curse began after the owner of the Boston _____
COLOR

_____ traded Babe _____, sometimes
PLURAL NOUN   LAST NAME

called the Bambino, to the New York _____ at the
PLURAL NOUN

end of the 1919 season. Before the trade, the team was playing

_____, winning its first ever World _____
ADVERB   PLURAL NOUN

and dominating the game. But after the trade, things went

_____ wrong. They failed to win another
ADVERB

_____ for the next eighty-six years and endured
NOUN

many _____-breaking losses. New York, to whom the Bambino
PART OF THE BODY

was _____ traded, went on a decades-long _____
ADVERB   VERB ENDING IN "ING"

streak and dominated the American _____, winning
NOUN

more _____ than any other team. The Babe went
PLURAL NOUN

down in history as one of the greatest _____
PLURAL NOUN

of all time. They say that Boston spent the money from the sale

of the Bambino to pay for a theatrical production titled, *No, No,*

_____! I hope it was a/an _____ show!
PERSON IN ROOM   ADJECTIVE

GOING, GOING, GONE!

ADJECTIVE

_____

ADJECTIVE

_____

NOUN

_____

PERSON IN ROOM

_____

NOUN

_____

PERSON IN ROOM

_____

ADJECTIVE

_____

VERB ENDING IN "ING"

_____

NOUN

_____

ADJECTIVE

_____

PART OF THE BODY

_____

NOUN

_____

PLURAL NOUN

_____

ARTICLE OF CLOTHING

_____

NOUN

_____

NOUN

_____

ADJECTIVE

_____

EXCLAMATION

_____

PLURAL NOUN

_____

MAD LIBS° is fun to play with friends, but you can also play it by yourself! To begin with, DO NOT look at the story on the page below. Fill in the blanks on this page with the words called for. Then, using the words you have selected, fill in the blank spaces in the story.

Now you've created your own hilarious MAD LIBS° game!

MAD LIBS

GOING, GOING, GONE!

A/An _____ sports commentary to be read aloud:
      ADJECTIVE

Announcer #1: Well it's a/an _____ day for baseball here at
                                  ADJECTIVE

_____ Park, and _____ is about to throw out
   NOUN   PERSON IN ROOM

the first _____.
            NOUN

Announcer #2: He's facing _____, who is a/an
                              PERSON IN ROOM

_____ hitter with a .325 _____ average.
   ADJECTIVE   VERB ENDING IN "ING"

Announcer #1: And here's the pitch. . . It's a/an _____-
                                                      NOUN

ball for strike one. The hitter doesn't look too _____ about it.
                                                  ADJECTIVE

He is shaking his _____ and stepping outside the batter's
                   PART OF THE BODY

_____ to collect his _____.
   NOUN   PLURAL NOUN

Announcer #2: The pitcher adjusts his _____ and
                                          ARTICLE OF CLOTHING

reads the signs from his catcher. He nods, he winds up, and here's the

_____ . . .
   NOUN

Announcer #1: It's a hit! Deep to right _____! It's going . . .
                                            NOUN

it's going . . . it's _____! _____! A home run for
                     ADJECTIVE   EXCLAMATION

the _____!
     PLURAL NOUN

MAD LIBS® is fun to play with friends, but you can also play it by yourself! To begin with, DO NOT look at the story on the page below. Fill in the blanks on this page with the words called for. Then, using the words you have selected, fill in the blank spaces in the story.

Now you've created your own hilarious MAD LIBS® game!

STICKBALL

ADJECTIVE _____

ADJECTIVE _____

VERB _____

PLURAL NOUN _____

NOUN _____

PLURAL NOUN _____

PART OF THE BODY (PLURAL) _____

PLURAL NOUN _____

NOUN _____

NOUN _____

NOUN _____

ADJECTIVE _____

PLURAL NOUN _____

NOUN _____

MAD LIBS®

STICKBALL

If you don't live near a/an _____ baseball field, you

ADJECTIVE

can always play stickball—a city version of baseball. You will need a/an

_____ stick, a rubber ball, and bases to _____

ADJECTIVE   VERB

around. A lot of things in the street can be used as bases:

sewers, manhole covers, and _____. You don't need

PLURAL NOUN

a pitcher in stickball—the players just toss the _____ in the

NOUN

air and hit it themselves. WARNING: You have to be careful not to hit

_____ parked along the sides of the road, and if you hit a fly

PLURAL NOUN

ball, keep your _____ crossed it doesn't

PART OF THE BODY (PLURAL)

go through any glass _____. Also, if possible, play on a/an

PLURAL NOUN

_____ with very little _____ traffic. As long

NOUN   NOUN

as you observe safety precautions, stickball can be just as much

_____ as the _____ game of baseball.

NOUN   ADJECTIVE

So get all your neighborhood _____ together and play

PLURAL NOUN

_____!

NOUN

MAD LIBS® is fun to play with friends, but you can also play it by yourself! To begin with, DO NOT look at the story on the page below. Fill in the blanks on this page with the words called for. Then, using the words you have selected, fill in the blank spaces in the story.

Now you've created your own hilarious MAD LIBS® game!

A LEAGUE OF THEIR OWN

_____ NOUN

_____ ADJECTIVE

_____ NOUN

_____ VERB

_____ ADJECTIVE

_____ NOUN

_____ A PLACE

_____ A PLACE

_____ PLURAL NOUN

_____ NOUN

_____ NOUN

_____ LAST NAME

_____ NOUN

_____ ADJECTIVE

_____ NOUN

_____ PLURAL NOUN

_____ NOUN

MAD LIBS®

A LEAGUE OF THEIR OWN

Did you know that there used to be a professional baseball

_____ for women? It was called the All-_____
         NOUN   ADJECTIVE

Girls Baseball League. When America entered _____
                                                                       NOUN

War II, most of the men went off to _____. In order to keep
                                                    VERB

professional baseball _____, some team owners decided
                                   ADJECTIVE

to make a/an _____ for women. Some team names were (the)
                        NOUN

_____ Daisies, (the) _____ Belles, and the
     A PLACE   A PLACE

Rockford _____. These _____-breaking
                   PLURAL NOUN   NOUN

women inspired a movie called *A/An* _____ *of Their*
                                                        NOUN

Own, which starred Tom _____ and won two
                                            LAST NAME

Golden _____ awards. The _____ players
              NOUN   ADJECTIVE

were all inducted into the Baseball _____ of Fame,
                                                     NOUN

and have become an inspiration to _____ everywhere.
                                                    PLURAL NOUN

It goes to show that you can accomplish anything if you set your

_____ to it!
       NOUN

MAD LIBS®

HOT OFF THE PRESSES
MAD LIBS

by Roger Price and Leonard Stern

INSTRUCTIONS

MAD LIBS® is a game for people who don't like games!
It can be played by one, two, three, four, or forty.

● RIDICULOUSLY SIMPLE DIRECTIONS

In this tablet you will find stories containing blank spaces where words are left out. One player, the READER, selects one of these stories. The READER does not tell anyone what the story is about. Instead, he/she asks the other players, the WRITERS, to give him/her words. These words are used to fill in the blank spaces in the story.

● TO PLAY

The READER asks each WRITER in turn to call out a word—an adjective or a noun or whatever the space calls for—and uses them to fill in the blank spaces in the story. The result is a MAD LIBS® game.

When the READER then reads the completed MAD LIBS® game to the other players, they will discover that they have written a story that is fantastic, screamingly funny, shocking, silly, crazy, or just plain dumb—depending upon which words each WRITER called out.

● EXAMPLE (*Before* and *After*)

"_____!" he said _____
     EXCLAMATION   ADVERB

as he jumped into his convertible _____ and
                                  NOUN

drove off with his _____ wife.
              ADJECTIVE

"*Ouch*!" he said *stupidly*
     EXCLAMATION   ADVERB

as he jumped into his convertible *cat* and
                                  NOUN

drove off with his *brave* wife.
              ADJECTIVE

QUICK REVIEW

In case you have forgotten what adjectives, adverbs, nouns, and verbs are, here is a quick review:

An ADJECTIVE describes something or somebody. *Lumpy, soft, ugly, messy,* and *short* are adjectives.

An ADVERB tells how something is done. It modifies a verb and usually ends in "ly." *Modestly, stupidly, greedily,* and *carefully* are adverbs.

A NOUN is the name of a person, place, or thing. *Sidewalk, umbrella, bridle, bathtub,* and *nose* are nouns.

A VERB is an action word. *Run, pitch, jump,* and *swim* are verbs. Put the verbs in past tense if the directions say PAST TENSE. *Ran, pitched, jumped,* and *swam* are verbs in the past tense.

When we ask for A PLACE, we mean any sort of place: a country or city (*Spain, Cleveland*) or a room (*bathroom, kitchen*).

An EXCLAMATION or SILLY WORD is any sort of funny sound, gasp, grunt, or outcry, like *Wow!, Ouch!, Whomp!, Ick!,* and *Gadzooks!*

When we ask for specific words, like a NUMBER, a COLOR, an ANIMAL, or a PART OF THE BODY, we mean a word that is one of those things, like *seven, blue, horse,* or *head.*

When we ask for a PLURAL, it means more than one. For example, *cat* pluralized is *cats.*

MAD LIBS® is fun to play with friends, but you can also play it by yourself! To begin with, DO NOT look at the story on the page below. Fill in the blanks on this page with the words called for. Then, using the words you have selected, fill in the blank spaces in the story.

Now you've created your own hilarious MAD LIBS® game!

BEHIND THE SCENES

ADJECTIVE _____

ADJECTIVE _____

VERB ENDING IN "ING" _____

A PLACE _____

ADJECTIVE _____

PLURAL NOUN _____

PLURAL NOUN _____

VERB _____

ADJECTIVE _____

PART OF THE BODY (PLURAL) _____

VERB _____

PART OF THE BODY _____

SILLY WORD _____

ADJECTIVE _____

PLURAL NOUN _____

MAD LIBS®

BEHIND THE SCENES

Putting on a newscast might look easy, but it takes a lot of _____

ADJECTIVE

work. Go behind the scenes, and you'll see dozens of _____ workers

ADJECTIVE

_____ in every direction! Reporters run back and forth between

VERB ENDING IN "ING"

the studio and locations all around (the) _____ to cover _____

A PLACE   ADJECTIVE

stories and interview _____. They are joined by videographers who

PLURAL NOUN

operate handheld _____ to capture all the action. The anchors are

PLURAL NOUN

the people who _____ behind the news desk and read the stories

VERB

during the newscast. They have to look _____ on air, so they can often

ADJECTIVE

be found getting makeup applied to their _____. The director

PART OF THE BODY (PLURAL)

tells everyone where and when to _____. It's easy to spot a director

VERB

because he wears a headset on his _____ and yells things like

PART OF THE BODY

"Camera two!" and "Cut to commercial!" and "_____!" A newscast

SILLY WORD

is live television, so if you make a/an _____ mistake, everyone

ADJECTIVE

watching at home on their _____ will know!

PLURAL NOUN

MAD LIBS® is fun to play with friends, but you can also play it by yourself! To begin with, DO NOT look at the story on the page below. Fill in the blanks on this page with the words called for. Then, using the words you have selected, fill in the blank spaces in the story.

Now you've created your own hilarious MAD LIBS® game!

TODAY'S TOP STORIES

_____ ADJECTIVE

_____ NOUN

_____ A PLACE

_____ ADJECTIVE

_____ PLURAL NOUN

_____ NOUN

_____ PERSON IN ROOM

_____ NUMBER

_____ PLURAL NOUN

_____ PERSON IN ROOM

_____ NOUN

_____ PLURAL NOUN

_____ ADJECTIVE

_____ PLURAL NOUN

_____ VERB ENDING IN "ING"

_____ PLURAL NOUN

_____ CELEBRITY (MALE)

_____ PERSON IN ROOM (FEMALE)

_____ ADJECTIVE

_____ A PLACE

MAD LIBS®
TODAY'S TOP STORIES

Good morning! Here are the _____ stories we're following today:
                               ADJECTIVE

• A thirty-foot-high _____ struck the coast of (the)
                            NOUN

   _____ earlier today, causing _____ flooding
          A PLACE   ADJECTIVE

   and forcing residents to flee to higher _____.
                                                PLURAL NOUN

• A rare watercolor _____ by renowned fifteenth-century artist
                           NOUN

   _____ Van Gogh sold at auction today for the record sum
      PERSON IN ROOM

   of _____ _____.
        NUMBER   PLURAL NOUN

• _____ turns 113 today and is declared the oldest living
      PERSON IN ROOM

   _____ by the *Book of World* _____.
          NOUN   PLURAL NOUN

• New, _____ research out of the University of _____
         ADJECTIVE   PLURAL NOUN

   concludes that thirty minutes of vigorous _____ can help
                                               VERB ENDING IN "ING"

   you lose up to ten _____ in a month.
                        PLURAL NOUN

• Hollywood heartthrob _____ has married longtime love
                          CELEBRITY (MALE)

   _____ in a lavish, _____ ceremony in (the)
   PERSON IN ROOM (FEMALE)   ADJECTIVE

   _____.
        A PLACE

A MORNING PERSON

ADJECTIVE
_____

NOUN
_____

A PLACE
_____

VERB ENDING IN "ING"
_____

ANIMAL (PLURAL)
_____

ADJECTIVE
_____

NOUN
_____

PERSON IN ROOM
_____

ADJECTIVE
_____

VERB ENDING IN "ING"
_____

CELEBRITY
_____

PERSON IN ROOM
_____

NOUN
_____

NUMBER
_____

PLURAL NOUN
_____

VERB
_____

MAD LIBS® is fun to play with friends, but you can also play it by yourself! To begin with, DO NOT look at the story on the page below. Fill in the blanks on this page with the words called for. Then, using the words you have selected, fill in the blank spaces in the story.

Now you've created your own hilarious MAD LIBS® game!

MAD LIBS®

A MORNING PERSON

Are you cheery and _____ at the crack of dawn? Do you leap out of bed
                         ADJECTIVE

early in the morning, ready to greet the world with a dazzling _____? As
                                                                NOUN

a journalist, can you quickly switch gears from interviewing the ruler of (the)

_____ to quizzing an expert on the effects of global _____
A PLACE   VERB ENDING IN "ING"

on the planet to judging a beauty contest for _____? Then *you*
                                               ANIMAL (PLURAL)

could be the _____ morning show host we're looking for! The number-
             ADJECTIVE

one–ranked show *Good Morning,* _____ is searching for a cohost
                                 NOUN

to join the current host, _____. The show combines
                          PERSON IN ROOM

_____, hard news stories with lighter pieces such as cooking and
ADJECTIVE

_____ segments, interviews with A-listers like _____
VERB ENDING IN "ING"   CELEBRITY

and _____, and fashion tips such as one hundred stylish ways to
    PERSON IN ROOM

wear a feathered _____. Salary is $_____ a year plus a
                 NOUN   NUMBER

generous allowance for clothing and _____. Are you qualified?
                                     PLURAL NOUN

Then _____ today for an application!
     VERB

BREAKING NEWS: ALIEN ABDUCTION

_____ NOUN

_____ ADJECTIVE

_____ A PLACE

_____ ADJECTIVE

_____ PERSON IN ROOM (FEMALE)

_____ NOUN

_____ ADJECTIVE

_____ NOUN

_____ TYPE OF LIQUID

_____ PLURAL NOUN

_____ PLURAL NOUN

_____ PART OF THE BODY (PLURAL)

_____ VERB (PAST TENSE)

_____ COLOR

_____ PART OF THE BODY (PLURAL)

_____ NOUN

_____ NOUN

_____ ADJECTIVE

_____ PART OF THE BODY (PLURAL)

MAD LIBS® is fun to play with friends, but you can also play it by yourself! To begin with, DO NOT look at the story on the page below. Fill in the blanks on this page with the words called for. Then, using the words you have selected, fill in the blank spaces in the story.

Now you've created your own hilarious MAD LIBS® game!

MAD LIBS

BREAKING NEWS: ALIEN ABDUCTION

The sighting of an unidentified flying _____ was confirmed yesterday
                                          NOUN

morning over the _____ skies of (the) _____. Later that evening,
                    ADJECTIVE   A PLACE

a/an _____ resident named _____ told police she had
       ADJECTIVE   PERSON IN ROOM (FEMALE)

been the victim of a/an _____ abduction! "_____ creatures
                             NOUN   ADJECTIVE

strapped me to a long _____ and made me drink something that
                          NOUN

looked like _____ but tasted like rotten _____," she revealed.
             TYPE OF LIQUID   PLURAL NOUN

"Then they taped _____ all over my _____, and their
                  PLURAL NOUN   PART OF THE BODY (PLURAL)

machines monitored me while I _____ nonstop for what seemed
                                VERB (PAST TENSE)

like hours!" She described the aliens as having large, _____
                                                         COLOR

_____ and moving very gracefully—almost like a winged
PART OF THE BODY (PLURAL)

_____ in flight. "Finally they placed me in a/an _____-shaped
   NOUN   NOUN

spacecraft and dropped me off in a/an _____ field," she said. "I wasn't
                                         ADJECTIVE

hurt, but I learned that I prefer my _____ planted firmly on the
                                       PART OF THE BODY (PLURAL)

ground!"

MAD LIBS® is fun to play with friends, but you can also play it by yourself! To begin with, DO NOT look at the story on the page below. Fill in the blanks on this page with the words called for. Then, using the words you have selected, fill in the blank spaces in the story.

Now you've created your own hilarious MAD LIBS® game!

ALL-ACCESS PRESS PASS

PERSON IN ROOM (FEMALE)_____

NOUN_____

NOUN_____

ADJECTIVE_____

COLOR_____

CELEBRITY (MALE)_____

PART OF THE BODY (PLURAL)_____

PERSON IN ROOM_____

ADJECTIVE_____

VERB (PAST TENSE)_____

ADJECTIVE_____

PLURAL NOUN_____

PLURAL NOUN_____

ADJECTIVE_____

PART OF THE BODY (PLURAL)_____

MAD LIBS®

ALL-ACCESS PRESS PASS

Hey there! _____ here, from WFUN-TV! Guess what? I was
            PERSON IN ROOM (FEMALE)

the lucky _____ assigned to cover the annual _____
              NOUN   NOUN

Awards and blog about it for you! So here are the _____ details!
                                                      ADJECTIVE

First, I hit the _____ carpet and snagged interviews with
                      COLOR

everyone from the delicious _____, who made me weak in the
                             CELEBRITY (MALE)

_____, to the current Hollywood "It" kid, _____,
PART OF THE BODY (PLURAL)   PERSON IN ROOM

who's every bit as _____ in person as in the movies! I
                        ADJECTIVE

_____ backstage for most of the show because that's where all the
VERB (PAST TENSE)

_____ action was. And the after parties were amazing! People were
    ADJECTIVE

toasting one another with glasses of chilled _____. Finally everyone
                                              PLURAL NOUN

jumped into their chauffeured _____ and sped home—everyone
                               PLURAL NOUN

except me, that is. Sadly, I had to use the only mode of transportation available to

a/an _____ reporter—my own two _____!
        ADJECTIVE   PART OF THE BODY (PLURAL)

From HOT OFF THE PRESSES MAD LIBS® • Copyright © 2012 by Penguin Random House LLC.

MAD LIBS® is fun to play with friends, but you can also play it by yourself! To begin with, DO NOT look at the story on the page below. Fill in the blanks on this page with the words called for. Then, using the words you have selected, fill in the blank spaces in the story.

Now you've created your own hilarious MAD LIBS® game!

SPORTS RECAP

NOUN_____

SILLY WORD_____

PART OF THE BODY_____

ADJECTIVE_____

NOUN_____

PLURAL NOUN_____

ADJECTIVE_____

PART OF THE BODY (PLURAL)_____

VERB_____

SAME VERB_____

PLURAL NOUN_____

PERSON IN ROOM_____

NOUN_____

ADJECTIVE_____

VERB ENDING IN "ING"_____

NOUN_____

PART OF THE BODY_____

NOUN_____

ADJECTIVE_____

ADJECTIVE_____

MAD LIBS®

SPORTS RECAP

It was the final game of the National _____-ball Championships,
NOUN

and—_____!—it was a/an _____-biter! The hometown team,
SILLY WORD   PART OF THE BODY

the _____ Mudslingers, was losing by just one _____. The
ADJECTIVE   NOUN

_____ were loaded, but the team was down to its last _____
PLURAL NOUN   ADJECTIVE

batter—and the final pitch. The sold-out crowd was on its _____,
PART OF THE BODY (PLURAL)

screaming "_____, Mudslingers, _____!" and waving giant
VERB   SAME VERB

foam _____. The pitch to star player _____ was
PLURAL NOUN   PERSON IN ROOM

perfect, and—*crack!*—the _____ was airborne. The _____
NOUN   ADJECTIVE

outfielder took off _____ toward the fence with his _____
VERB ENDING IN "ING"   NOUN

outstretched to catch the ball—but all he could do was watch it sail over his

_____ and into the stands. One _____ scored, then another!
PART OF THE BODY   NOUN

The crowd went absolutely _____! The Mudslingers won the game that
ADJECTIVE

day—and the hearts of their _____ fans forever!
ADJECTIVE

MAN ON THE STREET INTERVIEWS

A PLACE _____

ADJECTIVE _____

PERSON IN ROOM (FEMALE) _____

A PLACE _____

PLURAL NOUN _____

NOUN _____

NOUN _____

CELEBRITY _____

NOUN _____

PART OF THE BODY (PLURAL) _____

ADJECTIVE _____

PERSON IN ROOM _____

A PLACE _____

PART OF THE BODY _____

VERB _____

PERSON IN ROOM (MALE) _____

NOUN _____

MAD LIBS® is fun to play with friends, but you can also play it by yourself! To begin with, DO NOT look at the story on the page below. Fill in the blanks on this page with the words called for. Then, using the words you have selected, fill in the blank spaces in the story.

Now you've created your own hilarious MAD LIBS® game!

MAD LIBS®

MAN ON THE STREET INTERVIEWS

This is roving reporter Perry Winkle, and I'm here in (the) _____ to
                                                              A PLACE

ask folks today's random question: *What is the first thing you would do if you ruled*

the world? Responses ranged from intelligent to downright _____.
                                                                  ADJECTIVE

Here's a sampling:

- _____ from (the) _____ said, "I'd make
  PERSON IN ROOM (FEMALE)   A PLACE

  sure everyone had plenty of healthy _____ to eat and a warm,
                                        PLURAL NOUN

  safe _____ to live in."
       NOUN

- An up-and-coming _____ by the name of _____ said, "I
                     NOUN   CELEBRITY

  would give each man, woman, and _____ a job. It's important to
                                    NOUN

  use your mind or your _____ to work and make the world
                         PART OF THE BODY (PLURAL)

  a/an _____ place."
       ADJECTIVE

- _____ from (the) _____ said, "There'd be no wars.
  PERSON IN ROOM   A PLACE

  People would only be allowed to _____ wrestle one another, but
                                   PART OF THE BODY

  then they'd _____ and make up.
               VERB

- Local comedian _____ said, "I would require every citizen
                  PERSON IN ROOM (MALE)

  to address me by my superhero name—_____-man!"
                                       NOUN

MAD LIBS® is fun to play with friends, but you can also play it by yourself! To begin with, DO NOT look at the story on the page below. Fill in the blanks on this page with the words called for. Then, using the words you have selected, fill in the blank spaces in the story.

Now you've created your own hilarious MAD LIBS® game!

TRAFFIC REPORT

PLURAL NOUN _____

ADJECTIVE _____

VERB _____

NUMBER _____

NOUN _____

A PLACE _____

PLURAL NOUN _____

ADJECTIVE _____

PART OF THE BODY (PLURAL) _____

NOUN _____

CELEBRITY _____

ADJECTIVE _____

PLURAL NOUN _____

NOUN _____

PERSON IN ROOM _____

NOUN _____

NOUN _____

NOUN _____

MAD LIBS

TRAFFIC REPORT

Folks, I hate to be the bearer of bad _____, but it's a slow-go on today's
                           PLURAL NOUN

_____ roadways. Everyone seems to have forgotten how to _____
  ADJECTIVE   VERB

behind the wheel! There's a/an _____-_____ pileup on Route
                                 NUMBER   NOUN

86 that's got traffic backed up all the way to (the) _____! Police and
                                             A PLACE

emergency _____ are on the scene, but those _____
         PLURAL NOUN   ADJECTIVE

drivers craning their _____ to see what's going on aren't
                PART OF THE BODY (PLURAL)

helping matters. A car with a flat _____ is causing a slowdown on
                               NOUN

_____ Highway. A/An _____ semitruck headed downtown
   CELEBRITY   ADJECTIVE

has jackknifed, spilling its load of frozen _____. And here's something
                                  PLURAL NOUN

you don't see every day: A two-hundred-pound _____ by the
                                        NOUN

name of _____ escaped from the zoo and wandered into the path
     PERSON IN ROOM

of an oncoming _____, which then swerved and crashed into a/an
                NOUN

_____. Let's face it, folks—today's a day where you need patience, a
  NOUN

sense of humor, or a flying _____!
                  NOUN

From HOT OFF THE PRESSES MAD LIBS® • Copyright © 2012 by Penguin Random House LLC.

MAD LIBS® is fun to play with friends, but you can also play it by yourself! To begin with, DO NOT look at the story on the page below. Fill in the blanks on this page with the words called for. Then, using the words you have selected, fill in the blank spaces in the story.

Now you've created your own hilarious MAD LIBS® game!

THAT'S CLASSIFIED INFORMATION

ADJECTIVE_____

ADJECTIVE_____

NOUN_____

PERSON IN ROOM_____

ADJECTIVE_____

PLURAL NOUN_____

NUMBER_____

PLURAL NOUN_____

PLURAL NOUN_____

NOUN_____

NOUN_____

ADJECTIVE_____

PLURAL NOUN_____

NOUN_____

PLURAL NOUN_____

ADJECTIVE_____

PLURAL NOUN_____

MAD LIBS®

THAT'S CLASSIFIED INFORMATION

Got junk? Sell your unwanted stuff in our _____ classified section!
                                                    ADJECTIVE

Today's _____ deals include a/an:
           ADJECTIVE

• Baby grand _____ previously owned by legendary pianist
                      NOUN

  _____ " _____ Hands" O'Hara. Asking two thousand
  PERSON IN ROOM   ADJECTIVE

  _____ or best offer
  PLURAL NOUN

• _____-piece collection of rare_____finely crafted from ceramic,
  NUMBER   PLURAL NOUN

  porcelain, and gold-plated _____
                             PLURAL NOUN

• Cage, feeding bowl, and hand-knitted _____ for a pet
                                              NOUN

  _____
  NOUN

• _____ minifridge, perfect for holding bottles of _____
  ADJECTIVE   PLURAL NOUN

• Used pickup_____ with one hundred thousand _____
              NOUN   PLURAL NOUN

  and_____ bumper sticker stating "Honk if you love _____!"
      ADJECTIVE   PLURAL NOUN

MAD LIBS® is fun to play with friends, but you can also play it by yourself! To begin with, DO NOT look at the story on the page below. Fill in the blanks on this page with the words called for. Then, using the words you have selected, fill in the blank spaces in the story.

Now you've created your own hilarious MAD LIBS® game!

TALK SHOW QUEEN

NUMBER _____

NOUN _____

PERSON IN ROOM (FEMALE) _____

ADJECTIVE _____

PART OF THE BODY _____

NOUN _____

PERSON IN ROOM (MALE) _____

CELEBRITY (FEMALE) _____

PART OF THE BODY _____

NUMBER _____

NOUN _____

NOUN _____

ADJECTIVE _____

ADJECTIVE _____

A PLACE _____

After a/an _____-year reign as daytime TV's most popular talk show
                NUMBER

_____, _____ O'Walters finally announced her
   NOUN   PERSON IN ROOM (FEMALE)

retirement. On her _____ farewell show, she recalled the moments
                        ADJECTIVE

nearest and dearest to her _____:
                            PART OF THE BODY

- When famed Hollywood actor and leading _____,
                                              NOUN

  _____, proclaimed his love for _____—then
   PERSON IN ROOM (MALE)   CELEBRITY (FEMALE)

  surprised everyone by getting down on one _____ and proposing
                                             PART OF THE BODY

  with a/an _____-karat diamond _____.
             NUMBER   NOUN

- When a woman and the _____ she gave up for adoption twenty
                            NOUN

  years earlier were reunited.

- When each member of the _____ audience was given a fully
                              ADJECTIVE

  loaded, fuel-efficient _____ convertible and an all-expenses-paid
                            ADJECTIVE

  trip to (the) _____.
                  A PLACE

MAD LIBS® is fun to play with friends, but you can also play it by yourself! To begin with, DO NOT look at the story on the page below. Fill in the blanks on this page with the words called for. Then, using the words you have selected, fill in the blank spaces in the story.

Now you've created your own hilarious MAD LIBS® game!

BREAKING NEWS: BIGFOOT SPOTTED

_____ NOUN

_____ NOUN

_____ ADJECTIVE

_____ PART OF THE BODY

_____ NOUN

_____ PLURAL NOUN

_____ PLURAL NOUN

_____ PLURAL NOUN

_____ PERSON IN ROOM

_____ NOUN

_____ ANIMAL

_____ PART OF THE BODY (PLURAL)

_____ VERB ENDING IN "ING"

_____ VERB ENDING IN "ING"

_____ PART OF THE BODY

_____ PERSON IN ROOM

_____ VERB (PAST TENSE)

MAD LIBS®

BREAKING NEWS: BIGFOOT SPOTTED

A/An _____ Scout troop camping in a remote location inside
NOUN

_____ National Forest reported a/an _____ encounter
NOUN   ADJECTIVE

with the elusive creature known as Big-_____. "It was dusk. The
                                        PART OF THE BODY

_____ had just begun to set when we finished pitching our
NOUN

_____. We set out to gather _____ to make a fire
PLURAL NOUN   PLURAL NOUN

so we could roast some _____ for s'mores," said troop leader
                            PLURAL NOUN

_____. "We were just about to head back to camp when we heard
PERSON IN ROOM

a/an _____ snap loudly nearby. We figured it was a squirrel or a/an
        NOUN

_____, but then we saw a pair of _____
ANIMAL   PART OF THE BODY (PLURAL)

watching us from the darkness." The troop leader told how they took off

_____ as fast as they could through the forest and hid inside
VERB ENDING IN "ING"

their _____ bags all night. "I was scared out of my _____,"
    VERB ENDING IN "ING"   PART OF THE BODY

said nine-year-old _____. "I don't think I _____ more
                    PERSON IN ROOM   VERB (PAST TENSE)

than five minutes all night."

MAD LIBS® is fun to play with friends, but you can also play it by yourself! To begin with, DO NOT look at the story on the page below. Fill in the blanks on this page with the words called for. Then, using the words you have selected, fill in the blank spaces in the story.

Now you've created your own hilarious MAD LIBS® game!

CONCERT REVIEW

ADJECTIVE_____

COLOR_____

ANIMAL (PLURAL)_____

VERB ENDING IN "ING"_____

PLURAL NOUN_____

PERSON IN ROOM_____

PART OF THE BODY_____

PART OF THE BODY (PLURAL)_____

ADJECTIVE_____

PLURAL NOUN_____

ADJECTIVE_____

NOUN_____

VERB ENDING IN "ING"_____

ADJECTIVE_____

PERSON IN ROOM (FEMALE)_____

PART OF THE BODY_____

COLOR_____

ARTICLE OF CLOTHING_____

NOUN_____

PLURAL NOUN_____

MAD LIBS®

CONCERT REVIEW

The _____ _____ _____ performed
      ADJECTIVE   COLOR   ANIMAL (PLURAL)

last night and wowed the _____-room-only crowd of screaming
                         VERB ENDING IN "ING"

_____. Music Editor _____ was there and had this
  PLURAL NOUN   PERSON IN ROOM

to report:

"What a/an _____-blowing show! My _____ are
       PART OF THE BODY   PART OF THE BODY (PLURAL)

still ringing! The band performed all their _____ hits, like "Too Cool
                       ADJECTIVE

for _____" and "Best _____ Friends Forever." Between the
   PLURAL NOUN   ADJECTIVE

music and the awesome laser _____ show, the crowd was on its feet and
                NOUN

_____ to the beat the whole night. But the music and lights were
VERB ENDING IN "ING"

almost overshadowed by the many _____ costume changes by lead
                    ADJECTIVE

singer Lady _____. It was hard to decide which was
        PERSON IN ROOM (FEMALE)

more _____-dropping—the _____ leather
  PART OF THE BODY   COLOR

_____ and _____-shaped headpiece she wore or the
ARTICLE OF CLOTHING   NOUN

simple gown fashioned completely from _____."
                      PLURAL NOUN

MAD LIBS® is fun to play with friends, but you can also play it by yourself! To begin with, DO NOT look at the story on the page below. Fill in the blanks on this page with the words called for. Then, using the words you have selected, fill in the blank spaces in the story.

Now you've created your own hilarious MAD LIBS® game!

AND IN LOCAL NEWS

_____ ADJECTIVE

_____ NOUN

_____ PLURAL NOUN

_____ NOUN

_____ NOUN

_____ PERSON IN ROOM

_____ NOUN

_____ NOUN

_____ NOUN

_____ ADJECTIVE

_____ NOUN

_____ PLURAL NOUN

_____ PLURAL NOUN

_____ ADJECTIVE

_____ PLURAL NOUN

_____ NOUN

MAD LIBS®

AND IN LOCAL NEWS

Small-town life doesn't mean big things don't happen! Here are some of the

_____ events taking place this weekend and next in Little
    ADJECTIVE

_____ Falls:
    NOUN

• Stop by the Brotherhood of the _____ Lodge on Sunday for an all-
                  PLURAL NOUN

you-can-eat _____ breakfast to benefit the town's _____
          NOUN   NOUN

rescue shelter. Mayor _____ will be flipping hotcakes and grilling
                   PERSON IN ROOM

_____ patties.
    NOUN

• Join us for the grand opening of the town's first _____ Mart! A
                                        NOUN

limited edition _____ will be given away to the first one hundred
               NOUN

_____ shoppers.
    ADJECTIVE

• Next weekend is the annual _____ festival. Vendors will be selling
                          NOUN

fresh-picked _____, and baked _____ will be available. Come
          PLURAL NOUN   PLURAL NOUN

hungry—and leave _____!
             ADJECTIVE

• Mark your calendar for the community garage sale. Unearth your unused

_____ and sell them for a few bucks. Remember—one man's
    PLURAL NOUN

_____ is another man's treasure!
    NOUN

WARNING: SEVERE WEATHER

_____ ADJECTIVE

_____ A PLACE

_____ ADJECTIVE

_____ PLURAL NOUN

_____ PLURAL NOUN

_____ VERB ENDING IN "ING"

_____ NOUN

_____ ADJECTIVE

_____ NOUN

_____ NOUN

_____ PART OF THE BODY

_____ NOUN

_____ VERB ENDING IN "ING"

_____ TYPE OF LIQUID

_____ VERB

_____ PART OF THE BODY (PLURAL)

_____ ADJECTIVE

MAD LIBS® is fun to play with friends, but you can also play it by yourself! To begin with, DO NOT look at the story on the page below. Fill in the blanks on this page with the words called for. Then, using the words you have selected, fill in the blank spaces in the story.

Now you've created your own hilarious MAD LIBS® game!

MAD LIBS

WARNING: SEVERE WEATHER

Our radar shows a line of _____ weather stretching from the midwest
                    ADJECTIVE

plains all the way to the coast of (the) _____. This weather pattern is
                                    A PLACE

producing _____ thunderstorms with heavy rains, _____
           ADJECTIVE   PLURAL NOUN

gusting up to eighty mph, and hail the size of _____! Tornado
                                         PLURAL NOUN

warnings are in effect for most of the viewing area. A funnel cloud was spotted

_____ across an open field and destroying every _____
VERB ENDING IN "ING"   NOUN

in its path. Remember, in the event of a/an _____ tornado, head to
                                  ADJECTIVE

the basement or climb into the nearest _____ and pull a/an
                                      NOUN

_____ over you so that your _____ is protected. If
    NOUN   PART OF THE BODY

you're out driving around in your _____, be on the lookout for
                              NOUN

flash _____ in low-lying areas. If you get caught in rushing
      VERB ENDING IN "ING"

_____, climb out of your vehicle and _____ for
TYPE OF LIQUID   VERB

your life! Stay tuned to this channel—and keep your _____
                                PART OF THE BODY (PLURAL)

to the sky—for _____ weather-related updates.
        ADJECTIVE

HOW TO GET THE SCOOP

ADJECTIVE _____

ADJECTIVE _____

NOUN _____

VERB _____

NOUN _____

NOUN _____

PART OF THE BODY _____

ADJECTIVE _____

VERB ENDING IN "ING" _____

PLURAL NOUN _____

PLURAL NOUN _____

ADJECTIVE _____

NOUN _____

PLURAL NOUN _____

VERB ENDING IN "ING" _____

ADJECTIVE _____

MAD LIBS® is fun to play with friends, but you can also play it by yourself! To begin with, DO NOT look at the story on the page below. Fill in the blanks on this page with the words called for. Then, using the words you have selected, fill in the blank spaces in the story.

Now you've created your own hilarious MAD LIBS® game!

MAD LIBS®

HOW TO GET THE SCOOP

Do you have a/an _____ nose for news? Here are _____
          ADJECTIVE   ADJECTIVE

tips for becoming a/an _____-winning investigative journalist:
                          NOUN

1. March up to a person's front door and _____. When they answer
                                                VERB

    the _____, stick your micro-_____ right under their
            NOUN   NOUN

    _____ and start firing questions.
      PART OF THE BODY

2. Ask as many _____ questions as possible. Getting someone
                    ADJECTIVE

    to break down and start _____ is great.
                              VERB ENDING IN "ING"

3. Seek out a person's family and _____. Offer the large
                                        PLURAL NOUN

    amounts of _____ to tell you everything they know.
                  PLURAL NOUN

4. Assemble a/an _____ disguise to go undercover. An oversize
                      ADJECTIVE

    _____ to wear across your face and a fake pair of _____
          NOUN   PLURAL NOUN

    work well.

5. Practice _____ as fast as you can so, when necessary, you can
                VERB ENDING IN "ING"

    make a/an _____ getaway.
                  ADJECTIVE

SUMMER MOVIE REVIEWS

————————————— ADJECTIVE

————————————— NOUN

————————————— NOUN

————————————— PLURAL NOUN

————————————— PERSON IN ROOM (MALE)

————————————— ADJECTIVE

————————————— ADJECTIVE

————————————— PLURAL NOUN

————————————— ADJECTIVE

————————————— PERSON IN ROOM (MALE)

————————————— ANIMAL

————————————— SAME ANIMAL

————————————— ADJECTIVE

————————————— VERB

————————————— PERSON IN ROOM (FEMALE)

————————————— NOUN

————————————— ADJECTIVE

————————————— PLURAL NOUN

————————————— PERSON IN ROOM (MALE)

MAD LIBS® is fun to play with friends, but you can also play it by yourself! To begin with, DO NOT look at the story on the page below. Fill in the blanks on this page with the words called for. Then, using the words you have selected, fill in the blank spaces in the story.

Now you've created your own hilarious MAD LIBS® game!

MAD☺LIBS®

SUMMER MOVIE REVIEWS

It's summer, and you know what that means: _____ weather, icy-
                                          ADJECTIVE

cold _____-sicles, and big blockbusters. Check out what's coming to a/an
      NOUN

_____ near you this summer!
      NOUN

• _____ *of the Caribbean:* Captain _____ and his
      PLURAL NOUN   PERSON IN ROOM (MALE)

band of _____ scalawags take to the _____ seas in search of
         ADJECTIVE   ADJECTIVE

buried _____.
        PLURAL NOUN

• *The Big* _____ *Ogre:* A cranky ogre named _____,
            ADJECTIVE   PERSON IN ROOM (MALE)

his sidekick—a/an _____ named _____—and a/an
                   ANIMAL   SAME ANIMAL

_____ gang of fairy-tale creatures go on a search and _____
      ADJECTIVE   VERB

mission to rescue Princess _____ from a tower guarded by a fire-
                            PERSON IN ROOM (FEMALE)

breathing _____.
           NOUN

• *The Boy Wizard:* A/An _____ boy discovers he possesses magical
                          ADJECTIVE

_____ that he must use to defeat the evil wizard, Lord
      PLURAL NOUN

_____.
PERSON IN ROOM (MALE)

MAD LIBS® is fun to play with friends, but you can also play it by yourself! To begin with, DO NOT look at the story on the page below. Fill in the blanks on this page with the words called for. Then, using the words you have selected, fill in the blank spaces in the story.

Now you've created your own hilarious MAD LIBS® game!

CELEBRITY INTERVIEW

VERB _____

NOUN _____

PERSON IN ROOM _____

PART OF THE BODY _____

ADJECTIVE _____

NOUN _____

ADJECTIVE _____

NOUN _____

ADJECTIVE _____

ADJECTIVE _____

PLURAL NOUN _____

PART OF THE BODY _____

NOUN _____

ADJECTIVE _____

NUMBER _____

MAD LIBS®

CELEBRITY INTERVIEW

Movie critic Daisy Meadows had the chance to _____ with
                                                    VERB

international _____ star Brad Kluney and chat about his new
                  NOUN

project, *The* _____ *Chronicles.*
              PERSON IN ROOM

Daisy: Forgive me if I'm a bit _____-tied. I'm such a/an
                                    PART OF THE BODY

_____ fan of yours! You're the handsomest _____ I've ever
   ADJECTIVE   NOUN

laid eyes on.

Brad: That's so _____ of you to say.
                       ADJECTIVE

Daisy: So, Brad, in this movie, are you a good _____ or a/an
                                                        NOUN

_____ guy?
   ADJECTIVE

Brad: I play a/an _____ guy who gets mixed up with some _____
                        ADJECTIVE   PLURAL NOUN

who may or may not be on the wrong side of the law. I spend a lot of the movie

thoughtfully scratching my _____.
                            PART OF THE BODY

Daisy: There's already buzz that this role will earn you a/an _____
                                                                    NOUN

Award nomination.

Brad: A happy, _____ audience is all I want—and
                       ADJECTIVE

my _____-dollar salary.
      NUMBER

MAD LIBS® is fun to play with friends, but you can also play it by yourself! To begin with, DO NOT look at the story on the page below. Fill in the blanks on this page with the words called for. Then, using the words you have selected, fill in the blank spaces in the story.

Now you've created your own hilarious MAD LIBS® game!

BREAKING NEWS: LOST CITY FOUND

_____ ADJECTIVE

_____ A PLACE

_____ ADJECTIVE

_____ SILLY WORD

_____ PLURAL NOUN

_____ ADJECTIVE

_____ PLURAL NOUN

_____ PART OF THE BODY

_____ ANIMAL

_____ PART OF THE BODY

_____ ANIMAL

_____ CELEBRITY

_____ ADJECTIVE

_____ NOUN

_____ PERSON IN ROOM

_____ PART OF THE BODY (PLURAL)

MAD LIBS®

BREAKING NEWS: LOST CITY FOUND

A/An _____ archeological team working in the remote jungles of (the)
        ADJECTIVE

_____ have reportedly discovered the _____ ancient city of
    A PLACE   ADJECTIVE

_____ buried under about ten miles of _____. The team
   SILLY WORD   PLURAL NOUN

said they knew they had stumbled onto something _____ when they
                                                         ADJECTIVE

unearthed weapons, tools, and _____ handcrafted from pure gold
                                    PLURAL NOUN

and bearing the city's symbol—a mythical creature with the _____ of
                                                              PART OF THE BODY

a/an _____ and the _____ of a/an _____. If
       ANIMAL   PART OF THE BODY   ANIMAL

that weren't proof enough, Chief Archeologist Dr. _____ said they
                                                        CELEBRITY

were certain it was the ancient city when they found a tomb marked with the

name of the city's legendary, _____ ruler, Ah-Ah-Achooey-Kaboom-
                                  ADJECTIVE

Boom, which roughly translates to "one who sneezes as explosively as a/an _____
                                                                            NOUN

erupting." "It's incredible," said Junior Archeologist _____. "I never
                                                          PERSON IN ROOM

would have believed this place existed if I hadn't seen it with my own two

_____."
PART OF THE BODY (PLURAL)

DARE TO BE NEWSWORTHY

PLURAL NOUN _____

ADJECTIVE _____

PERSON IN ROOM (MALE) _____

NOUN _____

PLURAL NOUN _____

ARTICLE OF CLOTHING _____

PERSON IN ROOM (FEMALE) _____

COLOR _____

VERB (PAST TENSE) _____

PLURAL NOUN _____

PERSON IN ROOM (MALE) _____

NUMBER _____

PLURAL NOUN _____

PART OF THE BODY _____

A PLACE _____

A PLACE _____

PERSON IN ROOM (FEMALE) _____

CELEBRITY (MALE) _____

MAD LIBS® is fun to play with friends, but you can also play it by yourself! To begin with, DO NOT look at the story on the page below. Fill in the blanks on this page with the words called for. Then, using the words you have selected, fill in the blank spaces in the story.

Now you've created your own hilarious MAD LIBS® game!

MAD LIBS®

DARE TO BE NEWSWORTHY

Some people will do anything to get their fifteen minutes of _____.

PLURAL NOUN

Think you've seen it all? Check out the _____ things these people

ADJECTIVE

did to make headlines:

- _____, a star _____-ball player at his school,

PERSON IN ROOM (MALE)   NOUN

  ran a marathon wearing 5-inch stiletto _____ and a skintight,

PLURAL NOUN

  floral _____.

ARTICLE OF CLOTHING

- _____ painted herself bright _____ and

PERSON IN ROOM (FEMALE)   COLOR

  _____ in a public fountain while people blasted her with squirt

VERB (PAST TENSE)

  guns filled with _____.

PLURAL NOUN

- _____ tied _____ helium-filled

PERSON IN ROOM (MALE)   NUMBER

  _____ around his _____ and floated from (the)

PLURAL NOUN   PART OF THE BODY

  _____ to (the) _____.

A PLACE   A PLACE

- _____ walked up to every fast-food drive-through window

PERSON IN ROOM (FEMALE)

  in town and asked if she could have _____ to go.

CELEBRITY (MALE)

MAD LIBS® is fun to play with friends, but you can also play it by yourself! To begin with, DO NOT look at the story on the page below. Fill in the blanks on this page with the words called for. Then, using the words you have selected, fill in the blank spaces in the story.

Now you've created your own hilarious MAD LIBS® game!

POLITICAL DEBATE

ADJECTIVE   _____

COLOR   _____

NOUN   _____

ADJECTIVE   _____

VERB ENDING IN "ING"   _____

NOUN   _____

PLURAL NOUN   _____

ADJECTIVE   _____

PLURAL NOUN   _____

ADJECTIVE   _____

NOUN   _____

TYPE OF LIQUID   _____

MAD LIBS

POLITICAL DEBATE

Welcome to another edition of *Meet the* _____ *Candidates*! Today we
                                            ADJECTIVE

have Jessica and Justin from _____ Valley High School. Both of
                                  COLOR

them are running for student council _____. Let's listen as they share
                                          NOUN

their _____ ideas for leadership.
          ADJECTIVE

Jessica: I believe that teachers should assign _____ homework every
                                                VERB ENDING IN "ING"

night.

Justin: I will fight for the cafeteria's right to serve _____ tots every day
                                                          NOUN

at lunch and steamed _____ only once a week.
                        PLURAL NOUN

Jessica: I will make sure our library is stocked with the latest _____
                                                                  ADJECTIVE

best sellers.

Justin: I will keep our vending machines stocked with _____.
                                                        PLURAL NOUN

Jessica: A vote for me is a vote for a clean, safe, _____ school where
                                                      ADJECTIVE

each and every _____ can excel!
                  NOUN

Justin: A vote for me ensures drinking fountains are filled with clean, fresh

_____. Yum!
TYPE OF LIQUID

LOCAL HERO BECOMES SENSATION

PERSON IN ROOM (MALE) _____

ADJECTIVE _____

NOUN _____

A PLACE _____

VERB ENDING IN "ING" _____

NOUN _____

PLURAL NOUN _____

VERB _____

ADJECTIVE _____

PART OF THE BODY _____

NOUN _____

ADJECTIVE _____

NOUN _____

PART OF THE BODY _____

TYPE OF LIQUID _____

NOUN _____

PERSON IN ROOM (FEMALE) _____

PART OF THE BODY _____

NOUN _____

MAD LIBS®

LOCAL HERO BECOMES SENSATION

_____ "The Truck" MacAllister didn't consider himself a
PERSON IN ROOM (MALE)

hero—except when he made a/an _____ play on the _____-
ADJECTIVE   NOUN

ball field. But residents of (the) _____ begged to differ. MacAllister
A PLACE

happened to be _____ by a bank when a masked
VERB ENDING IN "ING"

_____ came running out carrying a bag of stolen _____.
NOUN   PLURAL NOUN

MacAllister didn't stop to _____—he just sprinted after the
VERB

_____ thief and tackled him. MacAllister held the robber in a/an
ADJECTIVE

_____-lock until police arrived. He didn't know that a pedestrian
PART OF THE BODY

had caught it all on video and posted it on _____-Tube. It was a/an
NOUN

_____ hit, and MacAllister became an overnight _____!
ADJECTIVE   NOUN

Strangers wanted to shake his _____. Restaurants gave him free
PART OF THE BODY

_____. A lovely _____ named _____
TYPE OF LIQUID   NOUN   PERSON IN ROOM (FEMALE)

even proposed marriage! But he never let fame go to his _____. "I'm
PART OF THE BODY

just a simple _____ who was in the right place at the right time," he
NOUN

said.

MAD LIBS®

MAD SCIENTIST
MAD LIBS

INSTRUCTIONS

MAD LIBS® is a game for people who don't like games!
It can be played by one, two, three, four, or forty.

• RIDICULOUSLY SIMPLE DIRECTIONS

In this tablet you will find stories containing blank spaces where words are left out. One player, the READER, selects one of these stories. The READER does not tell anyone what the story is about. Instead, he/she asks the other players, the WRITERS, to give him/her words. These words are used to fill in the blank spaces in the story.

• TO PLAY

The READER asks each WRITER in turn to call out a word—an adjective or a noun or whatever the space calls for—and uses them to fill in the blank spaces in the story. The result is a MAD LIBS® game.

When the READER then reads the completed MAD LIBS® game to the other players, they will discover that they have written a story that is fantastic, screamingly funny, shocking, silly, crazy, or just plain dumb—depending upon which words each WRITER called out.

• EXAMPLE (*Before* and *After*)

"_____!" he said _____
  EXCLAMATION   ADVERB

as he jumped into his convertible _____ and
                                              NOUN

drove off with his _____ wife.
                          ADJECTIVE

"_____*Ouch*_____!" he said _____*stupidly*_____
  EXCLAMATION   ADVERB

as he jumped into his convertible _____*cat*_____ and
                                              NOUN

drove off with his _____*brave*_____ wife.
                          ADJECTIVE

QUICK REVIEW

In case you have forgotten what adjectives, adverbs, nouns, and verbs are, here is a quick review:

An ADJECTIVE describes something or somebody. *Lumpy, soft, ugly, messy,* and *short* are adjectives.

An ADVERB tells how something is done. It modifies a verb and usually ends in "ly." *Modestly, stupidly, greedily,* and *carefully* are adverbs.

A NOUN is the name of a person, place, or thing. *Sidewalk, umbrella, bridle, bathtub,* and *nose* are nouns.

A VERB is an action word. *Run, pitch, jump,* and *swim* are verbs. Put the verbs in past tense if the directions say PAST TENSE. *Ran, pitched, jumped,* and *swam* are verbs in the past tense.

When we ask for A PLACE, we mean any sort of place: a country or city *(Spain, Cleveland)* or a room *(bathroom, kitchen).*

An EXCLAMATION or SILLY WORD is any sort of funny sound, gasp, grunt, or outcry, like *Wow!, Ouch!, Whomp!, Ick!,* and *Gadzooks!*

When we ask for specific words, like a NUMBER, a COLOR, an ANIMAL, or a PART OF THE BODY, we mean a word that is one of those things, like *seven, blue, horse,* or *head.*

When we ask for a PLURAL, it means more than one. For example, *cat* pluralized is *cats.*

MAD LIBS® is fun to play with friends, but you can also play it by yourself! To begin with, DO NOT look at the story on the page below. Fill in the blanks on this page with the words called for. Then, using the words you have selected, fill in the blank spaces in the story.

Now you've created your own hilarious MAD LIBS® game!

HOW TO GET MY LOOK, BY ALBERT EINSTEIN

_____ OCCUPATION

_____ ADVERB

_____ ADJECTIVE

_____ NOUN

_____ ADJECTIVE

_____ ADJECTIVE

_____ COLOR

_____ ADJECTIVE

_____ PART OF THE BODY

_____ NOUN

_____ ARTICLE OF CLOTHING

_____ OCCUPATION

MAD☺LIBS®
HOW TO GET MY LOOK,
BY ALBERT EINSTEIN

Hallo. I am famous _____ Albert Einstein. Some people say I
                    OCCUPATION

look _____ insane. And zey are right, I do! But I am not actually
     ADVERB

_____. Zis is just how I like to look. If you would also like to look
ADJECTIVE

like zis, use ze makeover tips I have outlined below.

- Never comb your _____: It is supposed to look like zis! The
                   NOUN

  more _____, the better, as I always say. It also helps if your hair
       ADJECTIVE

  is a/an _____ shade of _____.
          ADJECTIVE   COLOR

- Make _____ faces as often as possible. For example, stick out
        ADJECTIVE

  your _____ in pictures. Why? Because life is fun! Do zis when
       PART OF THE BODY

  your eager _____ students photograph you. Zey will love it!
             NOUN

- Always wear a white lab _____. Zis way, you will look
                          ARTICLE OF CLOTHING

  like a real _____.
              OCCUPATION

MAD LIBS® is fun to play with friends, but you can also play it by yourself! To begin with, DO NOT look at the story on the page below. Fill in the blanks on this page with the words called for. Then, using the words you have selected, fill in the blank spaces in the story.

Now you've created your own hilarious MAD LIBS® game!

THE BIOGRAPHY OF
ALBERT EINSTEIN

A PLACE _____

NUMBER _____

OCCUPATION _____

ADJECTIVE _____

COLOR _____

ADJECTIVE _____

ADVERB _____

ADVERB _____

PLURAL NOUN _____

PLURAL NOUN _____

VERB (PAST TENSE) _____

NOUN _____

NOUN _____

NOUN _____

PART OF THE BODY _____

A PLACE _____

MAD LIBS

THE BIOGRAPHY OF ALBERT EINSTEIN

Albert Einstein was born in (the) _____ in Germany in the year
                                   A PLACE

18-_____. He grew up to be a genius _____ with a/an
        NUMBER   OCCUPATION

_____ _____ head of hair and a/an _____ sense of
ADJECTIVE   COLOR   ADJECTIVE

humor. Even though he was _____ smart, the people who knew him
                               ADVERB

thought he acted pretty _____. He was notorious for losing
                              ADVERB

_____ and forgetting the _____ in his equations. Einstein
PLURAL NOUN   PLURAL NOUN

became famous for inventing things like E equals MC _____,
                                                        VERB (PAST TENSE)

the theory of _____, and the quantum _____ of light. In
                   NOUN   NOUN

1921, he won the Nobel _____ in Physics. After his death in 1955,
                             NOUN

Einstein's _____ was donated to (the) _____ Medical Center.
             PART OF THE BODY   A PLACE

QUIZ: ARE YOU A MAD SCIENTIST?

ADJECTIVE _____

ADJECTIVE _____

EXCLAMATION _____

ADJECTIVE _____

ADJECTIVE _____

VERB (PAST TENSE) _____

TYPE OF LIQUID _____

ANIMAL (PLURAL) _____

COLOR _____

ADJECTIVE _____

NOUN _____

NOUN _____

ADJECTIVE _____

ARTICLE OF CLOTHING _____

ADJECTIVE _____

OCCUPATION _____

MAD LIBS® is fun to play with friends, but you can also play it by yourself! To begin with, DO NOT look at the story on the page below. Fill in the blanks on this page with the words called for. Then, using the words you have selected, fill in the blank spaces in the story.

Now you've created your own hilarious MAD LIBS® game!

MAD☺LIBS®

QUIZ: ARE YOU A MAD SCIENTIST?

Are you crazy about science? Do you go nuts for _____ experiments?
                                              ADJECTIVE

Take this _____ quiz to find out if you're a mad scientist.
              ADJECTIVE

1. Your favorite saying is: a) "Oh, _____! What did I do?",
                                  EXCLAMATION

    b) "It's _____!", c) "This _____ experiment went exactly
               ADJECTIVE   ADJECTIVE

    as _____."
       VERB (PAST TENSE)

2. Your lab always contains: a) test tubes filled with _____,
                                           TYPE OF LIQUID

    b) _____ floating in jars, c) a few _____ mice in
       ANIMAL (PLURAL)   COLOR

    cages.

3. Your favorite thing to do at night is: a) go to bed and have _____
                                                  ADJECTIVE

    dreams, b) laugh maniacally while bringing to life an evil _____,
                                                     NOUN

    c) plan tomorrow's _____-work.
                              NOUN

If you answered mostly *B*s, guess what? You're a/an _____ scientist! Go
                                                    ADJECTIVE

put on your long white _____ and experiment in your
                          ARTICLE OF CLOTHING

_____ laboratory. If you answered mostly *A*s and *C*s, you're better off
   ADJECTIVE

as a/an _____!
          OCCUPATION

MAD LIBS® is fun to play with friends, but you can also play it by yourself! To begin with, DO NOT look at the story on the page below. Fill in the blanks on this page with the words called for. Then, using the words you have selected, fill in the blank spaces in the story.

Now you've created your own hilarious MAD LIBS® game!

LAB RAT ON THE LOOSE

SILLY WORD _____

ADJECTIVE _____

NUMBER _____

NOUN _____

VERB ENDING IN "ING" _____

NOUN _____

TYPE OF LIQUID _____

ADJECTIVE _____

PART OF THE BODY _____

ADJECTIVE _____

VERB ENDING IN "ING" _____

ADJECTIVE _____

ANIMAL _____

ADJECTIVE _____

MAD LIBS®

LAB RAT ON THE LOOSE

Uh-oh! Last night, _____ the lab rat escaped from his cage and ran
                    SILLY WORD

amok in the science lab. He was out to get revenge on the _____
                                                          ADJECTIVE

scientists who'd held him captive for _____ weeks. First, he ran straight
                                      NUMBER

to the _____ tubes and knocked them over, _____
        NOUN   VERB ENDING IN "ING"

glass all over the _____. Then he jumped into a vat of _____
                    NOUN   TYPE OF LIQUID

and left _____ _____-prints all over the floor. Later on, the
         ADJECTIVE   PART OF THE BODY

_____ rat finally got tired of _____ around and went
 ADJECTIVE   VERB ENDING IN "ING"

to sleep under a/an _____-scope. Looks like that silly _____
                    ADJECTIVE   ANIMAL

is finally done with all his _____ hijinks. For now, at least . . .
                             ADJECTIVE

From MAD SCIENTIST MAD LIBS® • Copyright © 2014 by Penguin Random House LLC.

MAD LIBS® is fun to play with friends, but you can also play it by yourself! To begin with, DO NOT look at the story on the page below. Fill in the blanks on this page with the words called for. Then, using the words you have selected, fill in the blank spaces in the story.

Now you've created your own hilarious MAD LIBS® game!

THE STORY OF
FRANKENSTEIN

PERSON IN ROOM (MALE)
_____

ADJECTIVE
_____

NOUN
_____

NOUN
_____

ADJECTIVE
_____

A PLACE
_____

PART OF THE BODY (PLURAL)
_____

NUMBER
_____

PLURAL NOUN
_____

NOUN
_____

ADJECTIVE
_____

NOUN
_____

ADJECTIVE
_____

A PLACE
_____

NOUN
_____

NOUN
_____

ADVERB
_____

VERB (PAST TENSE)
_____

MAD LIBS

THE STORY OF FRANKENSTEIN

Mary Shelley wrote a science-fiction book about a villainous mad scientist called

_____ Frankenstein. Frankenstein was a/an _____
PERSON IN ROOM (MALE)   ADJECTIVE

scientist from the nineteenth _____. His greatest wish was to one day
                                    NOUN

become a real _____. So he went to (the) _____ and took a brain,
                  NOUN   A PLACE

some _____, and _____ legs from several dead
        PART OF THE BODY (PLURAL)   NUMBER

_____. Once he had sewn the body parts together, Frankenstein
  PLURAL NOUN

used electricity to make the hideous _____ come to life. Soon, in the
                                          NOUN

middle of a/an _____ and stormy _____, the creature awoke!
                  ADJECTIVE   NOUN

It was Frankenstein's greatest creation, and one of the most _____
                                                                ADJECTIVE

beings to ever live—until it started terrorizing the citizens of (the) _____.
                                                                        A PLACE

Frankenstein had to take action. He armed himself with a/an _____
                                                                NOUN

and went on a hunt for the _____ he'd created. After searching
                              NOUN

_____ for months, Frankenstein finally had to give up his search
    ADVERB

because he _____.
              VERB (PAST TENSE)

From MAD SCIENTIST MAD LIBS® • Copyright © 2014 by Penguin Random House LLC.

MAD LIBS® is fun to play with friends, but you can also play it by yourself! To begin with, DO NOT look at the story on the page below. Fill in the blanks on this page with the words called for. Then, using the words you have selected, fill in the blank spaces in the story.

Now you've created your own hilarious MAD LIBS® game!

ANNOUNCEMENT: THE SCIENCE FAIR WINNERS

CITY _____

ADVERB _____

ADJECTIVE _____

PERSON IN ROOM (FEMALE) _____

NOUN _____

SILLY WORD _____

PERSON IN ROOM (MALE) _____

ADJECTIVE _____

VERB (PAST TENSE) _____

PERSON IN ROOM _____

VERB ENDING IN "ING" _____

NUMBER _____

COLOR _____

ADJECTIVE _____

NOUN _____

ADJECTIVE _____

MAD LIBS®
ANNOUNCEMENT:
THE SCIENCE FAIR WINNERS

Thank you all for participating in the _____ Middle School Science
CITY

Fair. Everyone worked very _____ on their projects and it shows. We
ADVERB

will now announce the first-, second-, and _____-place winners.
ADJECTIVE

_____ won first place for her miniature erupting
PERSON IN ROOM (FEMALE)

_____, which was a model of the largest volcano in history, Mount
NOUN

_____.
SILLY WORD

_____ got second place for his super _____ miniature
PERSON IN ROOM (MALE)   ADJECTIVE

solar system, in which all the planets _____ in circles.
VERB (PAST TENSE)

_____ was given a third-place ribbon for _____ an ant
PERSON IN ROOM   VERB ENDING IN "ING"

farm using sand and _____ tiny _____ ants.
NUMBER   COLOR

That's it for the _____ annual science fair. We'll see you next
ADJECTIVE

_____ for another round of _____ science experiments.
NOUN   ADJECTIVE

THE PERIODIC TABLE

PLURAL NOUN _____

NOUN _____

NOUN _____

ADJECTIVE _____

A PLACE _____

LAST NAME _____

PLURAL NOUN _____

NUMBER _____

NOUN _____

PLURAL NOUN _____

NOUN _____

LETTER OF THE ALPHABET _____

LETTER OF THE ALPHABET _____

PLURAL NOUN _____

VERB _____

MAD LIBS® is fun to play with friends, but you can also play it by yourself! To begin with, DO NOT look at the story on the page below. Fill in the blanks on this page with the words called for. Then, using the words you have selected, fill in the blank spaces in the story.

Now you've created your own hilarious MAD LIBS® game!

MAD LIBS

THE PERIODIC TABLE

The periodic table of _____ hangs in classrooms and _____
               PLURAL NOUN   NOUN

laboratories all around the _____. So what's this _____
                                NOUN   ADJECTIVE

chart all about? Well, in the eighteenth century, a chemist from (the)

_____ named Dmitry _____ created the very first
    A PLACE   LAST NAME

periodic table of _____. There are more than _____ elements
                   PLURAL NOUN   NUMBER

on the periodic table, organized by atomic _____. The elements all
                                      NOUN

have a certain number of protons, neutrons, and _____. Each
                                        PLURAL NOUN

element on the periodic _____ has a symbol that is often the first
                          NOUN

two letters of the element's name. For example, helium's symbol is

_____ _____. Some scientists say more
LETTER OF THE ALPHABET   LETTER OF THE ALPHABET

_____ should be added to the table. Maybe someday you'll
  PLURAL NOUN

_____ one yourself!
  VERB

MAD LIBS® is fun to play with friends, but you can also play it by yourself! To begin with, DO NOT look at the story on the page below. Fill in the blanks on this page with the words called for. Then, using the words you have selected, fill in the blank spaces in the story.

Now you've created your own hilarious MAD LIBS® game!

DR. JEKYLL AND MR. HYDE

_____ OCCUPATION

_____ CITY

_____ NOUN

_____ ADJECTIVE

_____ PLURAL NOUN

_____ VERB (PAST TENSE)

_____ ADJECTIVE

_____ ADVERB

_____ VERB

_____ PLURAL NOUN

_____ ADJECTIVE

_____ OCCUPATION

_____ NOUN

_____ NOUN

_____ ADJECTIVE

_____ NOUN

_____ ADJECTIVE

_____ TYPE OF LIQUID

_____ PART OF THE BODY

MAD LIBS

DR. JEKYLL AND MR. HYDE

Dr. Jekyll was a friendly old _____ living in _____, England.
OCCUPATION   CITY

Mr. Hyde was an evil young _____ who did _____ things to
NOUN   ADJECTIVE

every person he met. But these two _____ were also a lot alike.
PLURAL NOUN

They even kind of _____ the same! But Hyde had a/an
VERB (PAST TENSE)

_____ power over the doctor, and became _____ evil as time
ADJECTIVE   ADVERB

went on. He was willing to _____ anyone who got in his way, and even
VERB

took _____ from the _____ townspeople. Then Hyde
PLURAL NOUN   ADJECTIVE

murdered a well-known _____! But, what a surprise—it wasn't Hyde,
OCCUPATION

after all. It was Jekyll! They were the same exact _____. Turns out,
NOUN

Jekyll had split-_____ disorder. To fix this, Jekyll did _____
NOUN   ADJECTIVE

experiments on himself so that Hyde would leave his _____ once and
NOUN

for all. But the experiments were too _____. The chemicals and
ADJECTIVE

_____ didn't work. In the end, Hyde took over Jekyll's
TYPE OF LIQUID

_____, and Jekyll was never seen again.
PART OF THE BODY

From MAD SCIENTIST MAD LIBS® • Copyright © 2014 by Penguin Random House LLC.

LABORATORY SAFETY
DOS AND DON'TS

_____ PART OF THE BODY (PLURAL)

_____ NOUN

_____ ADVERB

_____ VERB ENDING IN "ING"

_____ NOUN

_____ VERB

_____ ADJECTIVE

_____ PART OF THE BODY (PLURAL)

_____ TYPE OF FOOD

_____ ADJECTIVE

_____ TYPE OF CONTAINER

_____ ANIMAL (PLURAL)

MAD LIBS® is fun to play with friends, but you can also play it by yourself! To begin with, DO NOT look at the story on the page below. Fill in the blanks on this page with the words called for. Then, using the words you have selected, fill in the blank spaces in the story.

Now you've created your own hilarious MAD LIBS® game!

MAD LIBS®

LABORATORY SAFETY DOS AND DON'TS

Do wear safety goggles. They will protect your _____ . **Don't**
<u>PART OF THE BODY (PLURAL)</u>

light anything on fire. Always keep a/an _____ extinguisher handy in
<u>NOUN</u>

case you _____ set your laboratory aflame. **Do** clean the lens of the
<u>ADVERB</u>

microscope before _____ it. You might think you're looking at
<u>VERB ENDING IN "ING"</u>

a cell when really you're just looking at piece of _____ . **Don't** get too
<u>NOUN</u>

close to the test tubes after combining their contents. They might _____
<u>VERB</u>

all over you! **Do** clean up after yourself. Experiments can leave you with

_____ hands and stinky _____ . **Don't** leave any
<u>ADJECTIVE</u> <u>PART OF THE BODY (PLURAL)</u>

experiments unattended. If you get hungry and want to grab a/an _____
<u>TYPE OF FOOD</u>

sandwich, stop! You need to stay put until the _____ chemicals
<u>ADJECTIVE</u>

in your beakers are done boiling and you've put them safely away in

a/an _____ . **Do** remember to feed your lab _____ .
<u>TYPE OF CONTAINER</u> <u>ANIMAL (PLURAL)</u>

They're not only your test subjects, they're your friends.

MAD LIBS® is fun to play with friends, but you can also play it by yourself! To begin with, DO NOT look at the story on the page below. Fill in the blanks on this page with the words called for. Then, using the words you have selected, fill in the blank spaces in the story.

Now you've created your own hilarious MAD LIBS® game!

I NEED A NEW LAB PARTNER!

PERSON IN ROOM (MALE) _____

ADJECTIVE _____

LAST NAME _____

PERSON IN ROOM (FEMALE) _____

ADJECTIVE _____

VERB (PAST TENSE) _____

NOUN _____

ADJECTIVE _____

NOUN _____

ADJECTIVE _____

ADJECTIVE _____

PLURAL NOUN _____

ADJECTIVE _____

MAD⊚LIBS®

I NEED A NEW LAB PARTNER!

To Whom It May Concern:

Hi. My name is _____, and I am looking for a new,
     PERSON IN ROOM (MALE)

_____ lab partner for Mrs. _____'s biology class. My last
 ADJECTIVE   LAST NAME

lab partner, _____, was really _____ and never
    PERSON IN ROOM (FEMALE)   ADJECTIVE

_____ our experiments on time. So I asked to switch, and the
 VERB (PAST TENSE)

teacher said if I wanted another _____ partner, I had to find one all
         NOUN

by myself. If you are smart, _____ in school, and always turn your
       ADJECTIVE

_____-work in on time, you'd be a/an _____ lab partner
 NOUN   ADJECTIVE

for me. Please only contact me if you're _____ about science and
          ADJECTIVE

love doing scientific _____. If this describes you, contact me at
     PLURAL NOUN

scienceluvr1@-_____-mail.com, or just find me by my locker after
    ADJECTIVE

lunch.

From MAD SCIENTIST MAD LIBS® • Copyright © 2014 by Penguin Random House LLC.

MAD LIBS® is fun to play with friends, but you can also play it by yourself! To begin with, DO NOT look at the story on the page below. Fill in the blanks on this page with the words called for. Then, using the words you have selected, fill in the blank spaces in the story.

Now you've created your own hilarious MAD LIBS® game!

MY WACKY
CHEMISTRY TEACHER

_____ LAST NAME

_____ PART OF THE BODY (PLURAL)

_____ NOUN

_____ EXCLAMATION

_____ PERSON IN ROOM (FEMALE)

_____ ADVERB

_____ NOUN

_____ ADJECTIVE

_____ NOUN

_____ EXCLAMATION

_____ VERB (PAST TENSE)

_____ NOUN

_____ ADJECTIVE

MAD LIBS®

MY WACKY CHEMISTRY TEACHER

There are a lot of rumors going around about Mr. _____, our
                                                    LAST NAME

chemistry teacher. He always has a crazy look in his _____.
                                                      PART OF THE BODY (PLURAL)

Sometimes, in the middle of a/an _____ lesson, he'll shout
                                  NOUN

"_____!" for no reason at all. My friend _____
   EXCLAMATION   PERSON IN ROOM (FEMALE)

told me that he acts _____ because one time during a/an _____-
                      ADVERB   NOUN

storm he was struck by lightning in his classroom. Ouch! That would probably

explain why he is so _____ all the time and shakes whenever he writes
                      ADJECTIVE

on the _____-board. Last week, while doing an experiment in class, he
         NOUN

yelled, "_____! It's alive!" and then _____ around the
          EXCLAMATION   VERB (PAST TENSE)

room holding a/an _____ full of mysterious bubbling liquid. Maybe
                   NOUN

the rumors are true; maybe my teacher really is _____!
                                                 ADJECTIVE

MAD LIBS® is fun to play with friends, but you can also play it by yourself! To begin with, DO NOT look at the story on the page below. Fill in the blanks on this page with the words called for. Then, using the words you have selected, fill in the blank spaces in the story.

Now you've created your own hilarious MAD LIBS® game!

AT-HOME EXPERIMENT #1: FLOATING PAPER CLIPS!

NUMBER _____

ADJECTIVE _____

ADJECTIVE _____

TYPE OF LIQUID _____

ADJECTIVE _____

ADVERB _____

NOUN _____

VERB ENDING IN "S" _____

VERB _____

PART OF THE BODY (PLURAL) _____

MAD LIBS®
AT-HOME EXPERIMENT
#1: FLOATING PAPER CLIPS!

Materials:

_____ paper clips
NUMBER

A piece of _____ paper
ADJECTIVE

A see-through _____-size bowl
ADJECTIVE

A pencil

Instructions:

1. Fill the bowl with _____.
    TYPE OF LIQUID

2. Rip a/an _____ piece of tissue paper and _____ drop it
    ADJECTIVE   ADVERB

    onto the water.

3. Drop one of the _____ clips onto the tissue paper.
    NOUN

4. Use the pencil to gently nudge the tissue paper until the paper clip

    _____.
    VERB ENDING IN "S"

5. If you do this just right, the paper clip will start to _____ in front
    VERB

    of your very _____!
    PART OF THE BODY (PLURAL)

FAMOUS SCIENTISTS

PLURAL NOUN _____

ADJECTIVE _____

NOUN _____

ADJECTIVE _____

VERB _____

NOUN _____

ADJECTIVE _____

SILLY WORD _____

PLURAL NOUN _____

ADJECTIVE _____

VERB (PAST TENSE) _____

ADVERB _____

ANIMAL _____

PLURAL NOUN _____

Now you've created your own hilarious MAD LIBS® game!

MAD LIBS® is fun to play with friends, but you can also play it by yourself! To begin with, DO NOT look at the story on the page below. Fill in the blanks on this page with the words called for. Then, using the words you have selected, fill in the blank spaces in the story.

MAD LIBS®

FAMOUS SCIENTISTS

Over the years, many famous _____ have developed _____
                              PLURAL NOUN   ADJECTIVE
theories, inventions, and ideas that have contributed to the evolution of

_____-kind. Below are some of the most _____ scientists to
      NOUN   ADJECTIVE
ever _____.
        VERB

Galileo Galilei was an Italian _____ who invented telescopes and found
                                        NOUN
out a lot of information about the _____ Way Galaxy, the solar system,
                                        ADJECTIVE
and planets like Jupiter and _____.
                                 SILLY WORD

Sir Isaac Newton discovered most of what we now know about gravity. He also

wrote scientific _____ called the First Law of Motion, the Second
                    PLURAL NOUN
Law of Motion, and the _____ Law of Motion.
                            ADJECTIVE

Charles Darwin invented theories about natural selection, which proved how

different species _____ over hundreds of years on Earth. He
                      VERB (PAST TENSE)
_____ studied several species of _____ on the Galapagos
      ADVERB   ANIMAL
_____.
   PLURAL NOUN

MAD LIBS® is fun to play with friends, but you can also play it by yourself! To begin with, DO NOT look at the story on the page below. Fill in the blanks on this page with the words called for. Then, using the words you have selected, fill in the blank spaces in the story.

Now you've created your own hilarious MAD LIBS® game!

TURN YOUR BEDROOM INTO A SECRET LAB

ADJECTIVE _____

ADJECTIVE _____

VERB ENDING IN "ING" _____

NOUN _____

VERB _____

PLURAL NOUN _____

NOUN _____

ADJECTIVE _____

TYPE OF CONTAINER (PLURAL) _____

TYPE OF LIQUID _____

ADVERB _____

ADJECTIVE _____

VERB ENDING IN "ING" _____

Follow these _____ steps to turn your boring, _____ bedroom
                 ADJECTIVE   ADJECTIVE

into a fully _____ science lab! First, put a big _____ on
            VERB ENDING IN "ING"   NOUN

your bedroom door that reads KEEP OUT! Scientists need to _____ in
                                                              VERB

silence without any annoying _____ interrupting them. Then clear off
                              PLURAL NOUN

your _____. You'll need it to hold all your oozy, _____
        NOUN   ADJECTIVE

chemicals. Gather a bunch of _____ and put them all over
                          TYPE OF CONTAINER (PLURAL)

your desk. Connect them with tubing so you can watch all the _____
                                                              TYPE OF LIQUID

run through them—_____ cool! Finally, pull your curtains shut—
                     ADVERB

you don't want anyone to see what kind of _____ concoctions
                                              ADJECTIVE

you're _____!
      VERB ENDING IN "ING"

MAD LIBS® is fun to play with friends, but you can also play it by yourself! To begin with, DO NOT look at the story on the page below. Fill in the blanks on this page with the words called for. Then, using the words you have selected, fill in the blank spaces in the story.

Now you've created your own hilarious MAD LIBS® game!

THE MAD SCIENTIST'S
SHOPPING LIST

PLURAL NOUN _____

PART OF THE BODY _____

ARTICLE OF CLOTHING _____

VERB ENDING IN "ING" _____

ANIMAL (PLURAL) _____

PLURAL NOUN _____

NOUN _____

ADJECTIVE _____

VERB _____

NOUN _____

MAD LIBS

THE MAD SCIENTIST'S SHOPPING LIST

- Long, rubbery black _____ to wear on your hands

PLURAL NOUN

- Giant round _____-glasses with black frames

PART OF THE BODY

- Long white lab _____

ARTICLE OF CLOTHING

- Two beakers—one to hold in each hand while _____

VERB ENDING IN "ING"

  maniacally

- Several cages for all your lab _____

ANIMAL (PLURAL)

- Assorted _____ floating in formaldehyde to add to your

PLURAL NOUN

  collection

- A chalkboard and a piece of _____ to write down your

NOUN

  _____ hypotheses and equations

ADJECTIVE

- A giant electrical power switch to turn on when you need to

  _____ something to life

VERB

- A Bunsen burner to light every _____ on fire!

NOUN

MAD LIBS® is fun to play with friends, but you can also play it by yourself! To begin with, DO NOT look at the story on the page below. Fill in the blanks on this page with the words called for. Then, using the words you have selected, fill in the blank spaces in the story.

Now you've created your own hilarious MAD LIBS® game!

MORE FAMOUS SCIENTISTS

ADJECTIVE _____

ADJECTIVE _____

NOUN _____

PLURAL NOUN _____

PERSON IN ROOM (MALE) _____

OCCUPATION _____

NOUN _____

VERB _____

NOUN _____

PLURAL NOUN _____

COLOR _____

NOUN _____

MAD LIBS®
MORE FAMOUS SCIENTISTS

Here are a few more _____ scientists!
ADJECTIVE

Nikola Tesla was born in Croatia. Later, he moved to the _____ States
ADJECTIVE

of America and became an inventor. He helped create fluorescent _____-
NOUN

bulbs so that people wouldn't have to use _____ to light their homes.
PLURAL NOUN

Tesla also invented radio and worked with _____ Edison to invent
PERSON IN ROOM (MALE)

things that helped electricity work.

Alexander Graham Bell was a/an _____ from the nineteenth century.
OCCUPATION

His mother was deaf, as was his _____. Because of this, Bell was
NOUN

interested in speech and hearing. He decided to create something that would help

people _____ each other, no matter where they were. He invented the
VERB

tele-_____ so that people could talk to one another.
NOUN

Stephen Hawking is a British physicist who studies galaxies and solar

_____. He has discovered a lot about _____ holes. His
PLURAL NOUN   COLOR

most famous book is called *A Brief History of* _____.
NOUN

MAD LIBS® is fun to play with friends, but you can also play it by yourself! To begin with, DO NOT look at the story on the page below. Fill in the blanks on this page with the words called for. Then, using the words you have selected, fill in the blank spaces in the story.

Now you've created your own hilarious MAD LIBS® game!

FRANKENSTEIN'S MONSTER

_____ NUMBER

_____ NOUN

_____ ADJECTIVE

_____ COLOR

_____ NOUN

_____ PLURAL NOUN

_____ PART OF THE BODY

_____ PART OF THE BODY

_____ ADJECTIVE

_____ VERB (PAST TENSE)

_____ ARTICLE OF CLOTHING

_____ ADJECTIVE

_____ ADJECTIVE

_____ NOUN

MAD LIBS®

FRANKENSTEIN'S MONSTER

Frankenstein's monster was a hideous, _____-foot-tall _____.
NUMBER   NOUN

His skin was a/an _____ shade of _____, his head was shaped
                        ADJECTIVE   COLOR

like a/an _____, and he had _____ sticking out of both
              NOUN   PLURAL NOUN

sides of his neck. Frankenstein's monster also had black lips and spiky black

hair on his _____, and his _____ was filled with
              PART OF THE BODY   PART OF THE BODY

big white teeth. His _____ arms stuck straight out whenever he
                          ADJECTIVE

_____ down the street, because the black shirt and
  VERB (PAST TENSE)

_____ he always wore were too small on his grotesque,
  ARTICLE OF CLOTHING

_____ body. What a/an _____-looking _____ he was!
  ADJECTIVE   ADJECTIVE   NOUN

MAD LIBS® is fun to play with friends, but you can also play it by yourself! To begin with, DO NOT look at the story on the page below. Fill in the blanks on this page with the words called for. Then, using the words you have selected, fill in the blank spaces in the story.

Now you've created your own hilarious MAD LIBS® game!

AT-HOME EXPERIMENT #2:
ERUPTING VOLCANO!

NOUN _____

ADJECTIVE _____

COLOR _____

VERB ENDING IN "ING" _____

TYPE OF LIQUID _____

ADJECTIVE _____

NOUN _____

PLURAL NOUN _____

ADJECTIVE _____

NUMBER _____

VERB _____

Materials:

A homemade volcano made out of plaster or _____-mâché

NOUN

A small _____ container

ADJECTIVE

_____ or yellow food coloring

COLOR

_____ soda

VERB ENDING IN "ING"

_____

TYPE OF LIQUID

Dish soap

Instructions:

1. Put the _____ container at the top of your volcano.

ADJECTIVE

2. Pour in a little bit of baking soda and some dish _____.

NOUN

3. Add a few _____ of _____ food coloring.

PLURAL NOUN   ADJECTIVE

4. Pour in _____ ounces of vinegar.

NUMBER

5. Watch your volcano _____ with lava!

VERB

THE WORST SCI-FI NIGHTMARE I EVER HAD

OCCUPATION
_____

PART OF THE BODY
_____

ADJECTIVE
_____

PLURAL NOUN
_____

VERB
_____

ADJECTIVE
_____

NOUN
_____

PART OF THE BODY (PLURAL)
_____

VERB
_____

COLOR
_____

TYPE OF LIQUID
_____

NOUN
_____

ADJECTIVE
_____

Now you've created your own hilarious MAD LIBS® game!

MAD LIBS® is fun to play with friends, but you can also play it by yourself! To begin with, DO NOT look at the story on the page below. Fill in the blanks on this page with the words called for. Then, using the words you have selected, fill in the blank spaces in the story.

I had a dream last night that a crazy _____ was trying to perform
OCCUPATION

experiments on me. He took a strand of my _____ and looked at it
PART OF THE BODY

under a microscope. Then he told me to sit in his _____ chair. But I was
ADJECTIVE

scared—there were a bunch of electrical _____ tied to it, and I was
PLURAL NOUN

afraid he was going to _____ me in it! I said, "No, thanks, you
VERB

_____ scientist—I'm getting the _____ out of here." He
ADJECTIVE   NOUN

looked me right in the _____ and said, "Don't you dare try to
PART OF THE BODY (PLURAL)

leave my dungeon! You can't _____—the door's locked!" Suddenly, he
VERB

pounced on me, and everything turned to _____. I woke up with
COLOR

_____ running down my temples. Thank _____ that
TYPE OF LIQUID   NOUN

nightmare is over. I hope I never see that _____ scientist ever again!
ADJECTIVE

MAD LIBS® is fun to play with friends, but you can also play it by yourself! To begin with, DO NOT look at the story on the page below. Fill in the blanks on this page with the words called for. Then, using the words you have selected, fill in the blank spaces in the story.

Now you've created your own hilarious MAD LIBS® game!

AT-HOME EXPERIMENT #3:
TORNADO IN A BOTTLE!

NOUN _____

VERB ENDING IN "ING" _____

VERB _____

ADJECTIVE _____

ADJECTIVE _____

VERB _____

NOUN _____

ADJECTIVE _____

NOUN _____

NOUN _____

ADJECTIVE _____

VERB (PAST TENSE) _____

MAD LIBS®

AT-HOME EXPERIMENT #3: TORNADO IN A BOTTLE

Materials:

Water

A see-through plastic soda ______________ with a cap
NOUN

Glitter, to see debris ______________ in the bottle
VERB ENDING IN "ING"

Dish soap to make your tornado ______________
VERB

Instructions:

1. Fill the entire ______________ bottle with water until it is almost all the
ADJECTIVE
way ______________.
ADJECTIVE

2. ______________ a few drops of dish ______________ into the bottle. Add
VERB NOUN
the ______________ glitter.
ADJECTIVE

3. Screw the ______________ onto the top of the bottle.
NOUN

4. Turn the bottle upside ______________ and hold it near the cap.
ADJECTIVE

5. Spin the bottle in a/an ______________-wise rotation.
NOUN

6. Stop spinning the bottle and admire the ______________ tornado you
ADJECTIVE
______________!
VERB (PAST TENSE)

From MAD SCIENTIST MAD LIBS® • Copyright © 2014 by Penguin Random House LLC.

MAD LIBS® is fun to play with friends, but you can also play it by yourself! To begin with, DO NOT look at the story on the page below. Fill in the blanks on this page with the words called for. Then, using the words you have selected, fill in the blank spaces in the story.

Now you've created your own hilarious MAD LIBS® game!

THE FIRST WEEK OF
SCIENCE CLASS

ADJECTIVE _____

LAST NAME _____

PLURAL NOUN _____

PLURAL NOUN _____

NOUN _____

NOUN _____

ANIMAL (PLURAL) _____

PERSON IN ROOM _____

ADJECTIVE _____

VERB _____

THE FIRST WEEK OF SCIENCE CLASS

My first few days of science class were so _____! Our teacher, Miss
_____ ADJECTIVE _____, taught us all about matter and energy, atoms and
_____ LAST NAME

_____, and the difference between solids, _____, and gases.
PLURAL NOUN   PLURAL NOUN

We even got to watch a video about gravity and why things in outer _____
                                                                      NOUN

float but things on Earth fall to the _____! Our teacher says that next
                                           NOUN

week we're going to do our first experiment and that, if we want, some day this

year we can even dissect _____! My friend _____ thought
                              ANIMAL (PLURAL)   PERSON IN ROOM

dissecting sounded gross, but I think it sounds really _____! I can't wait
                                                              ADJECTIVE

to _____ more about science next week.
        VERB